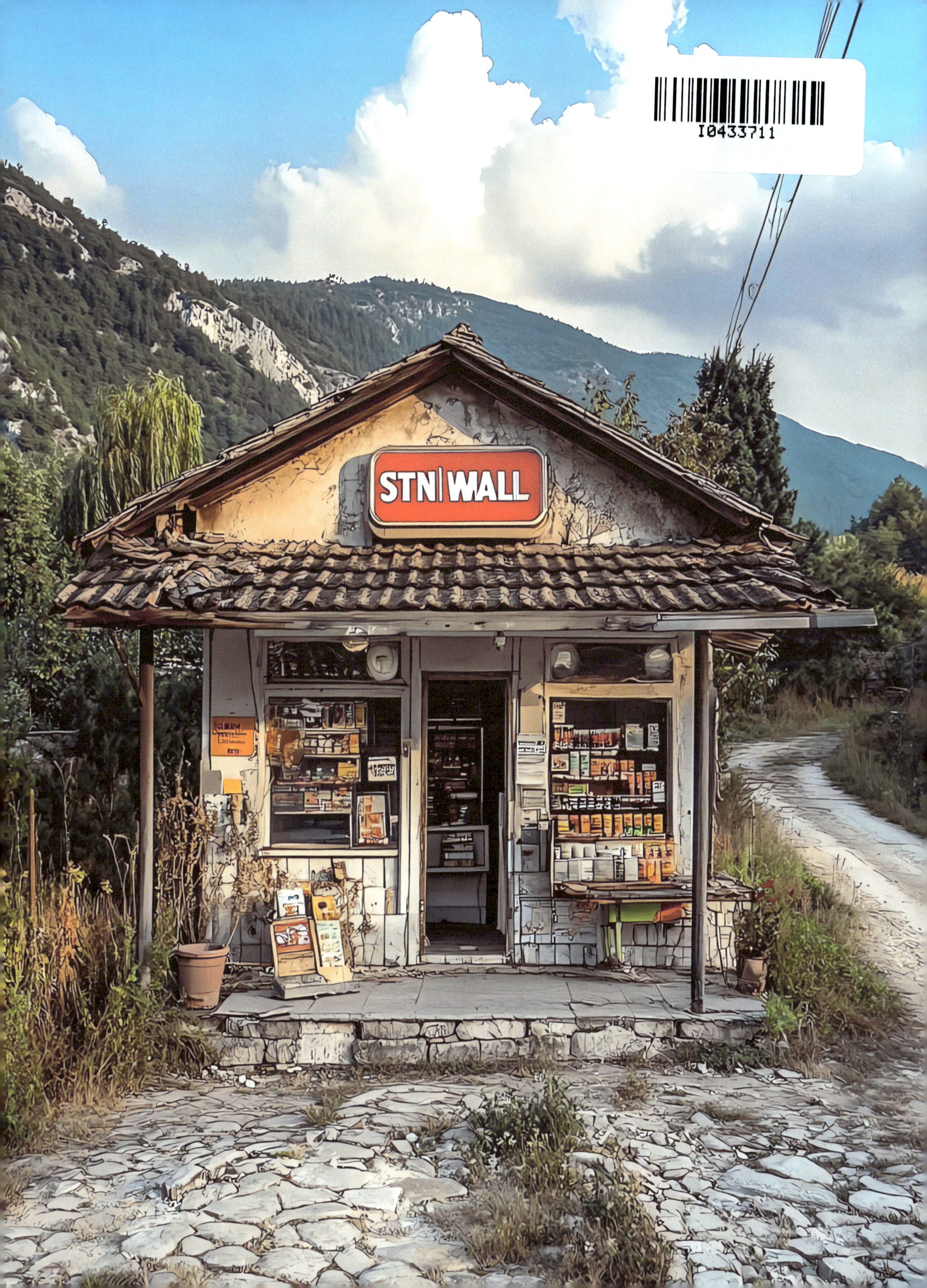
STN|WALL

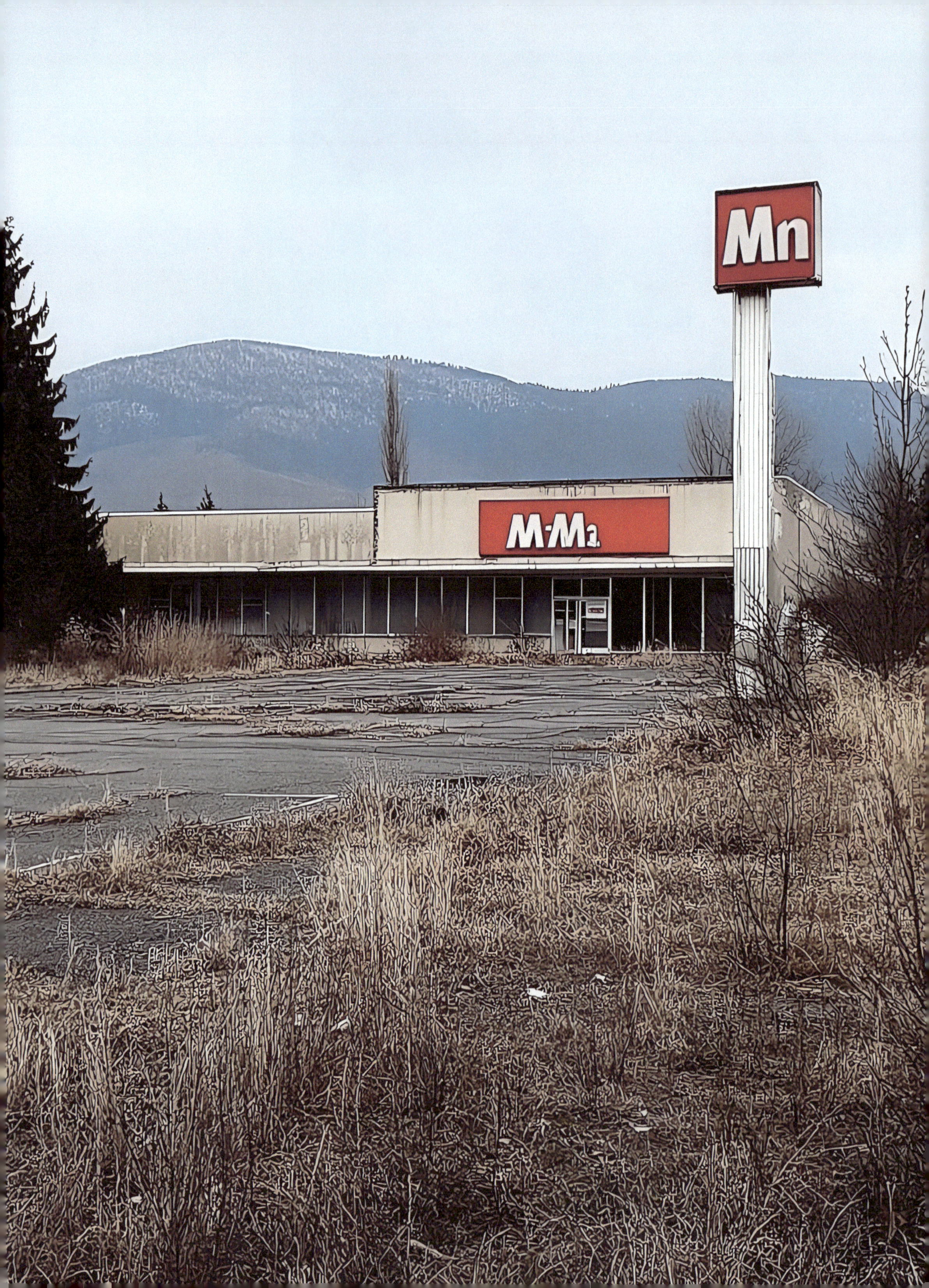
Mn
M-Ma.

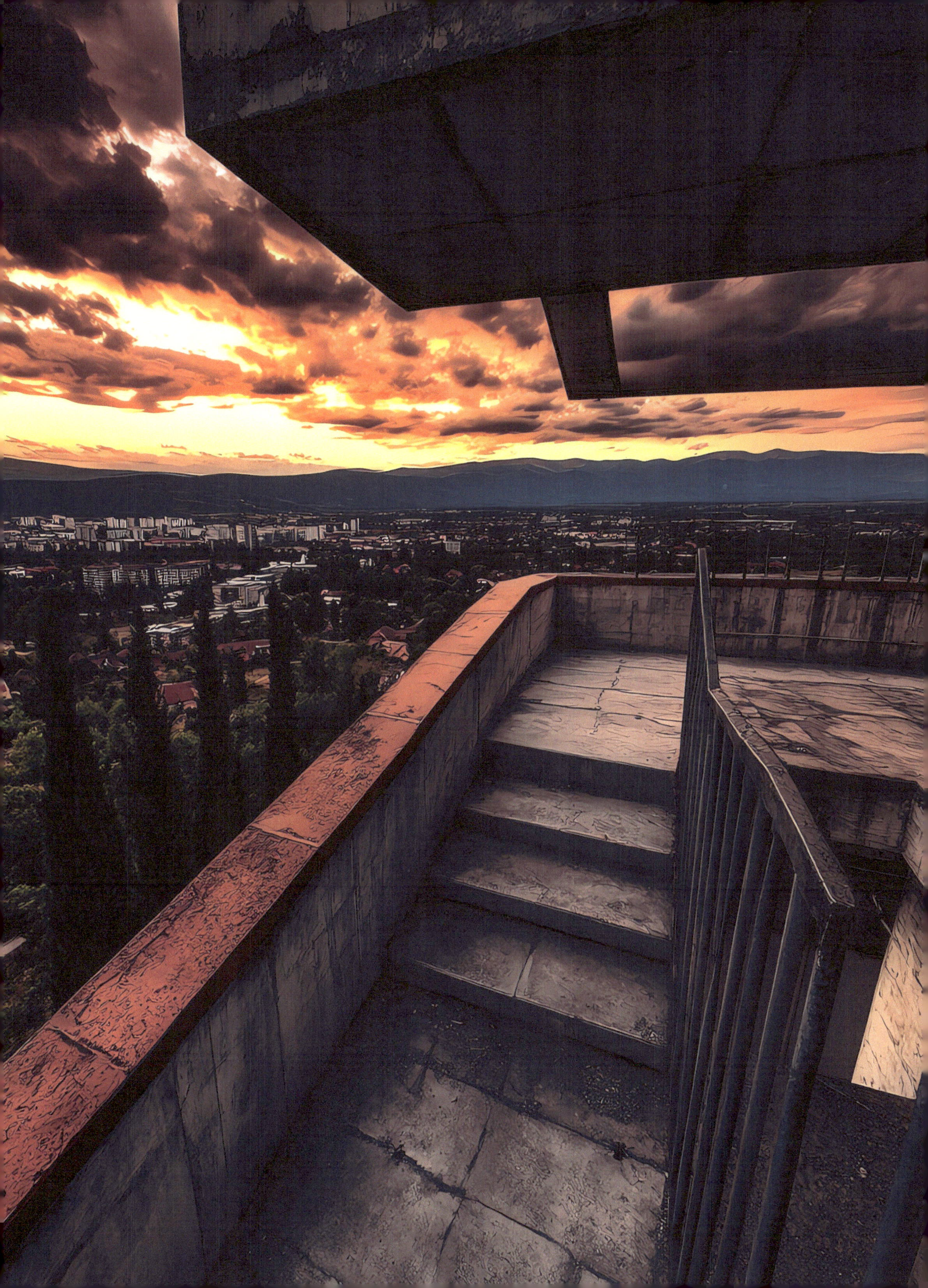

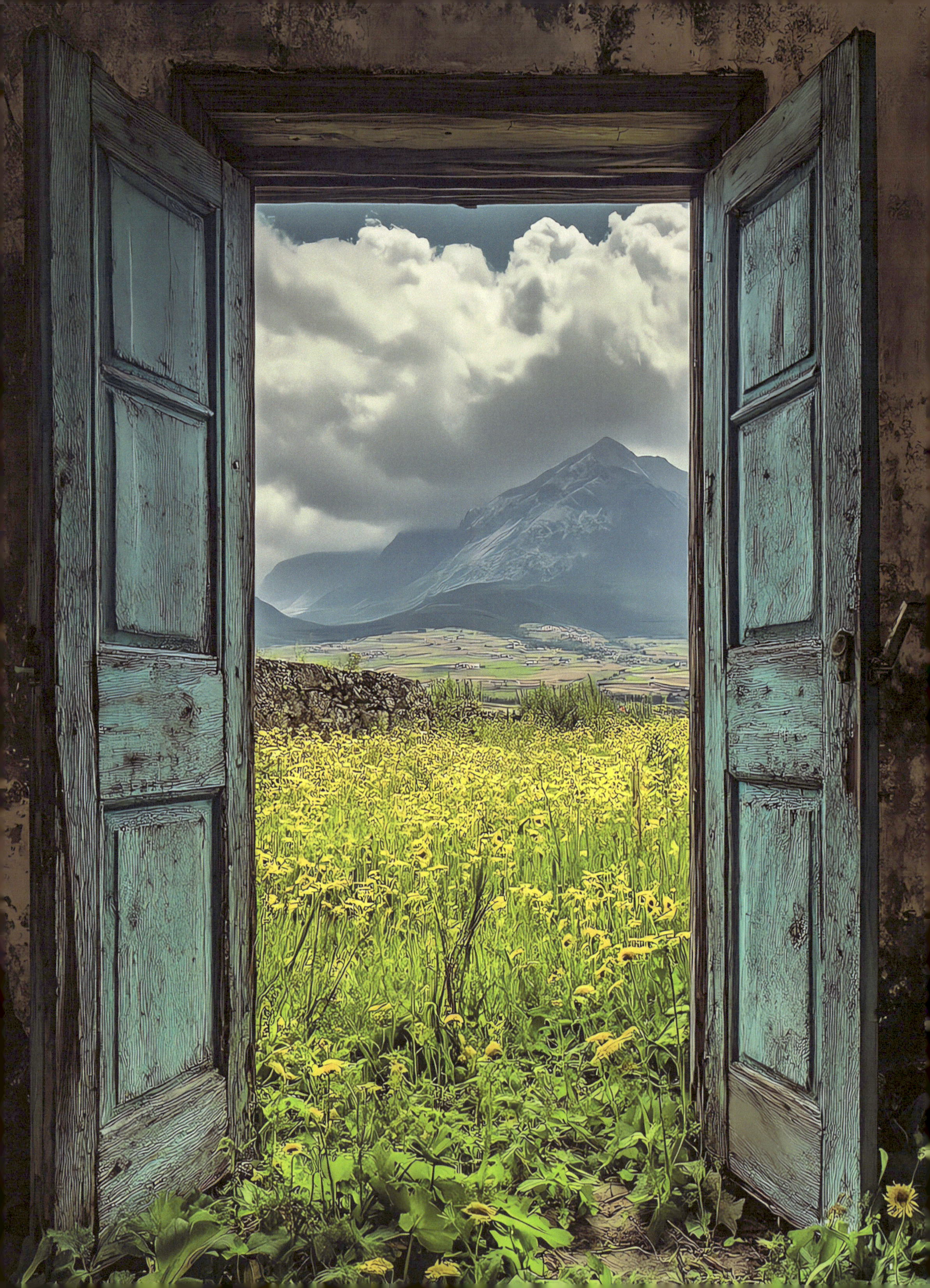

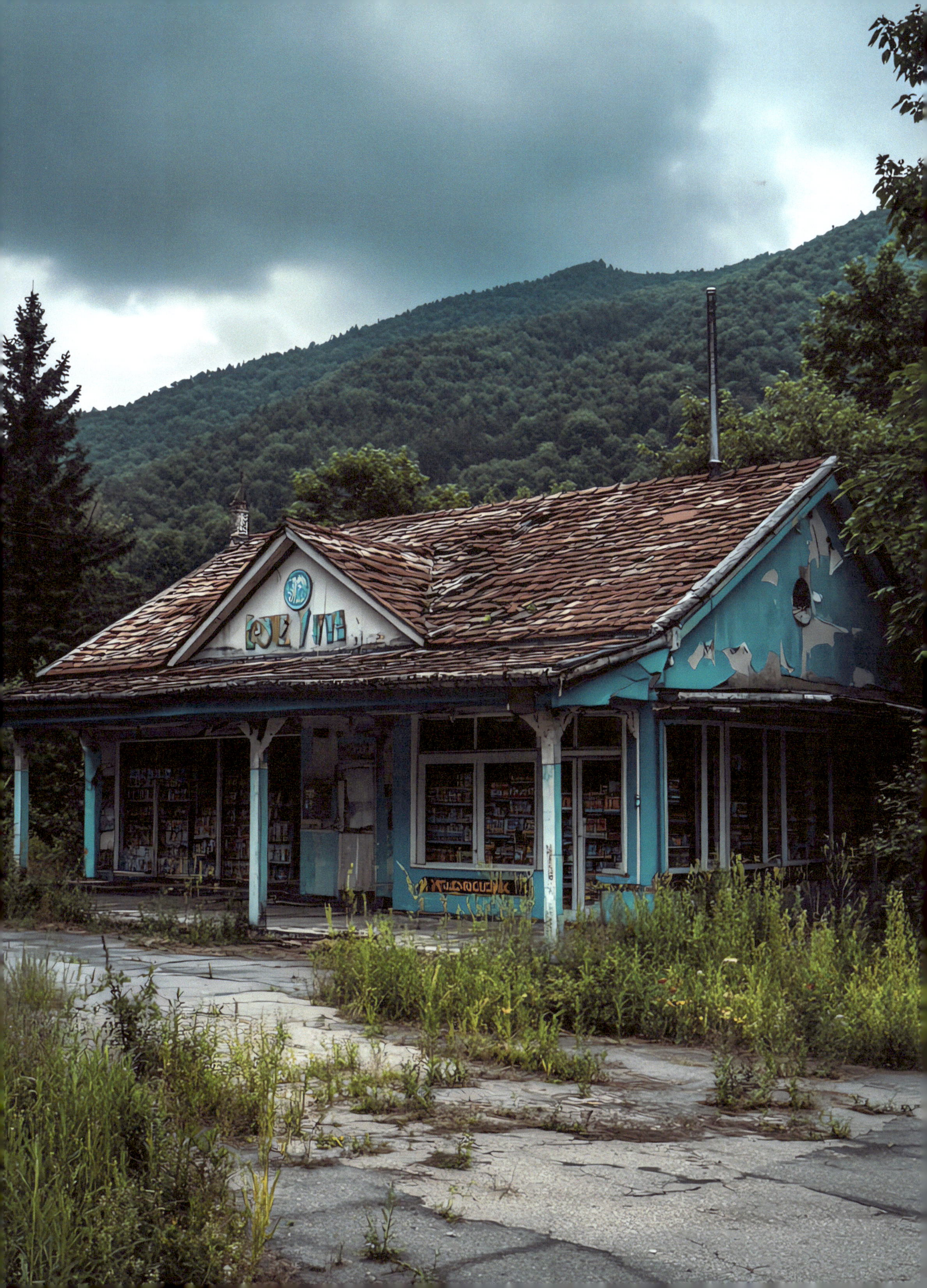

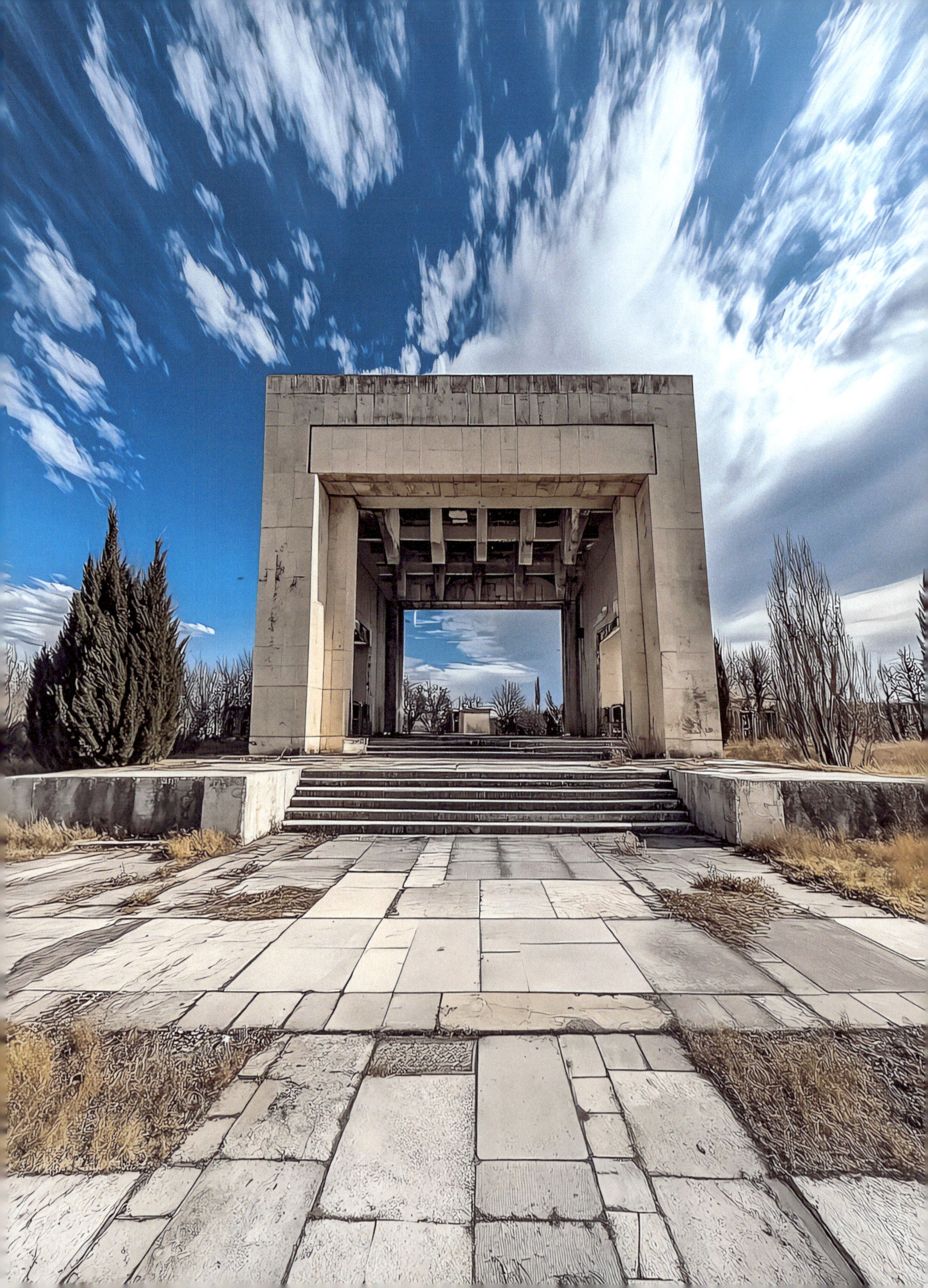

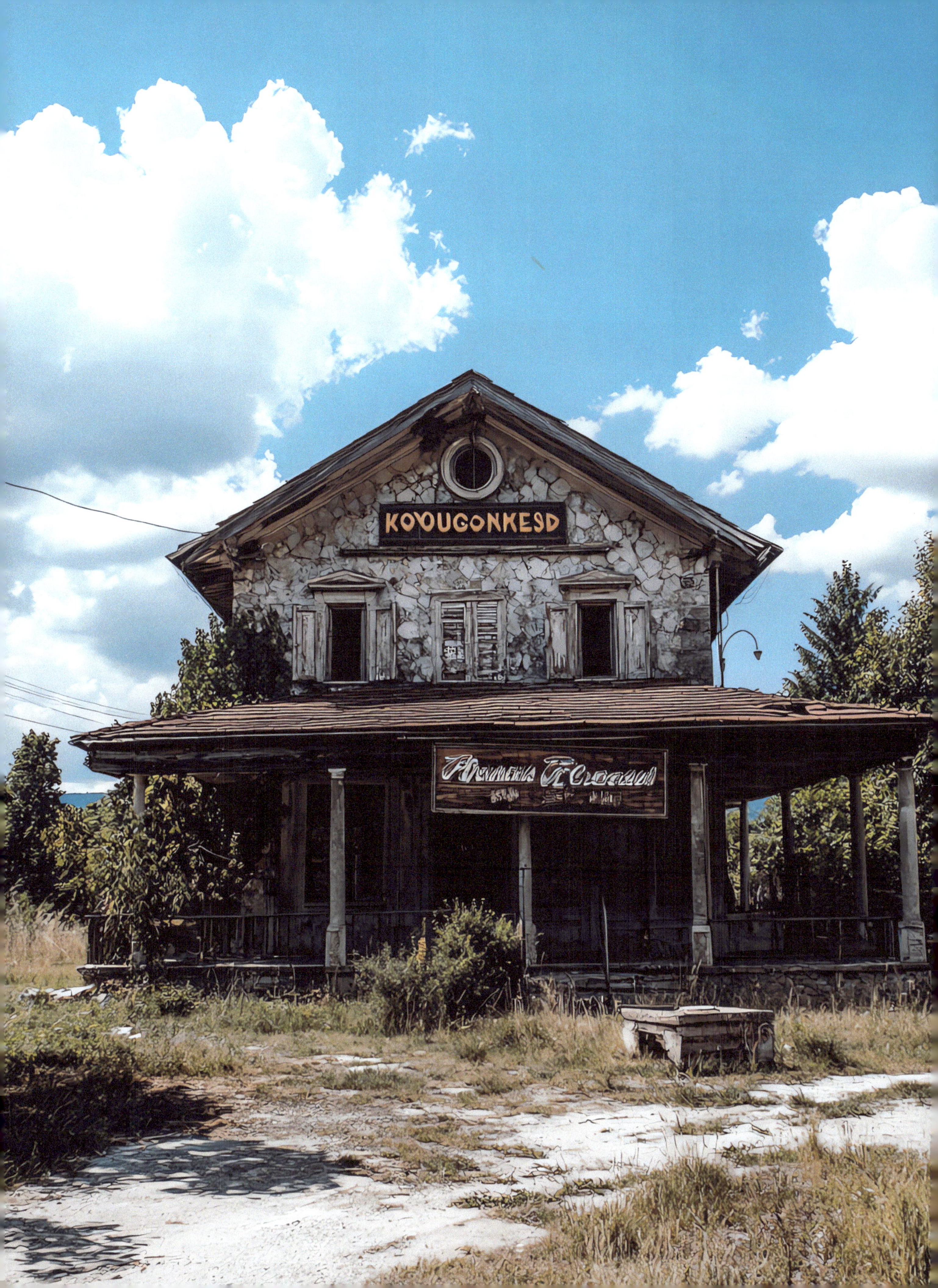
KOYOUGONKESD

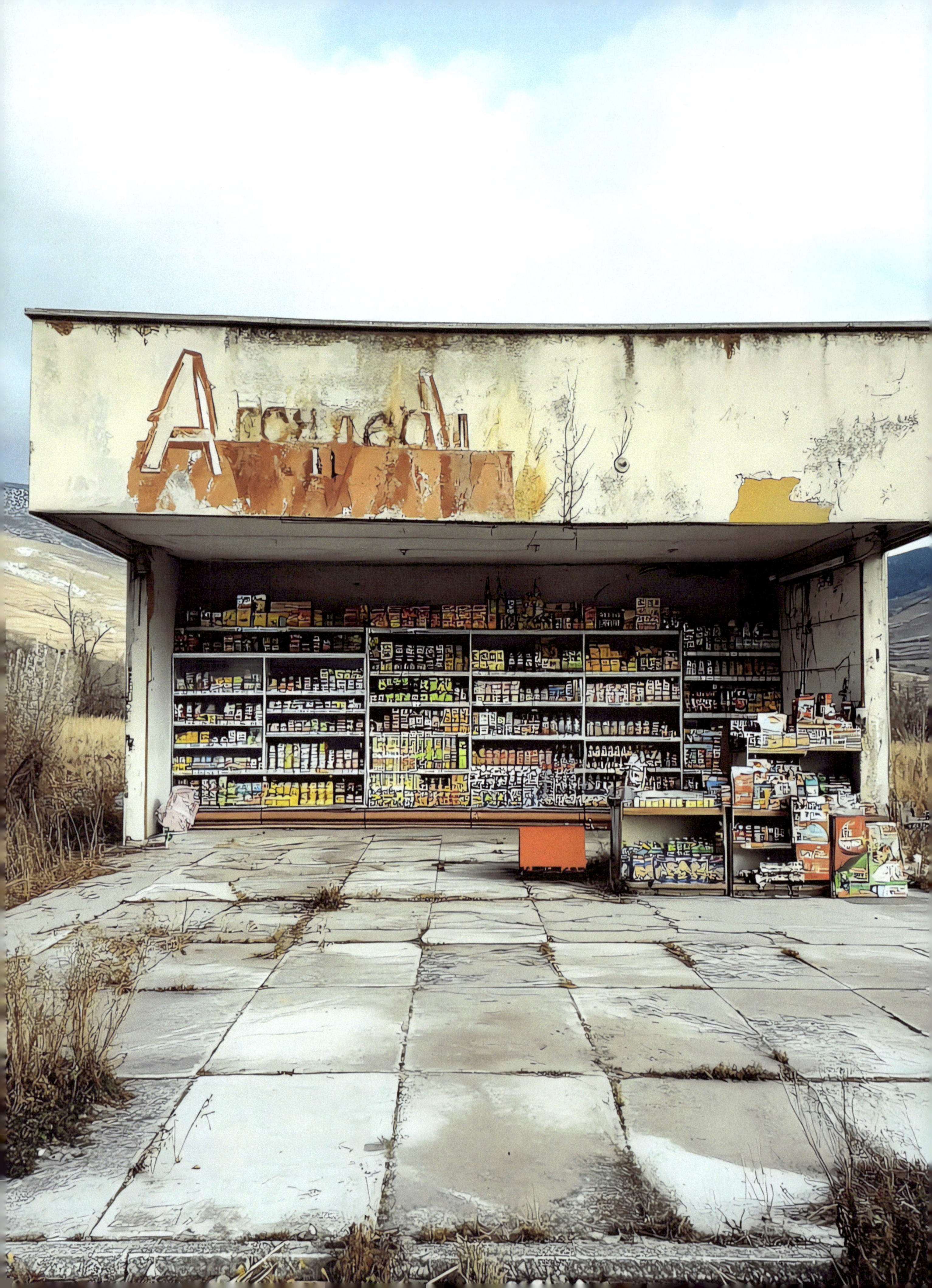

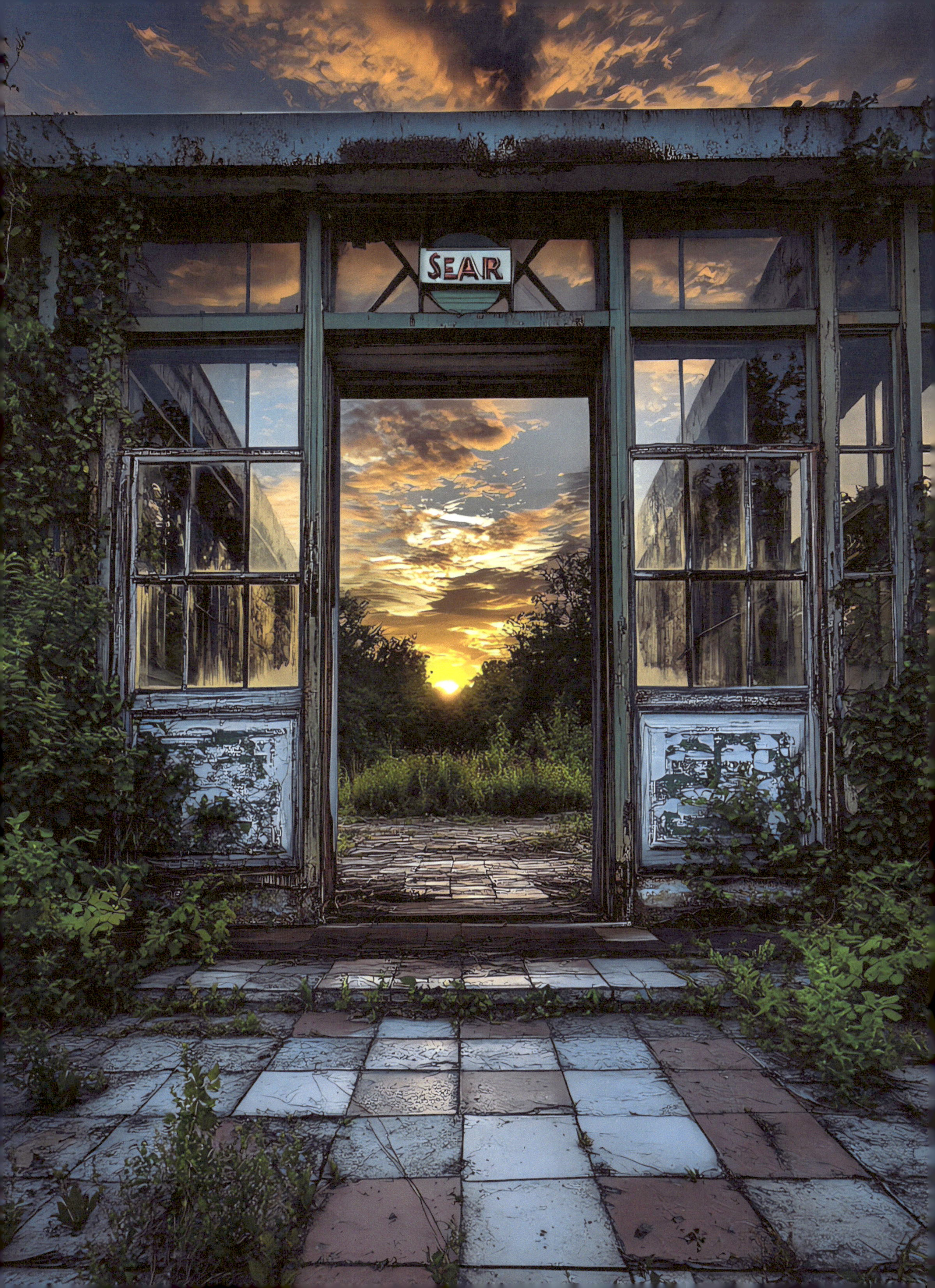
SEAR

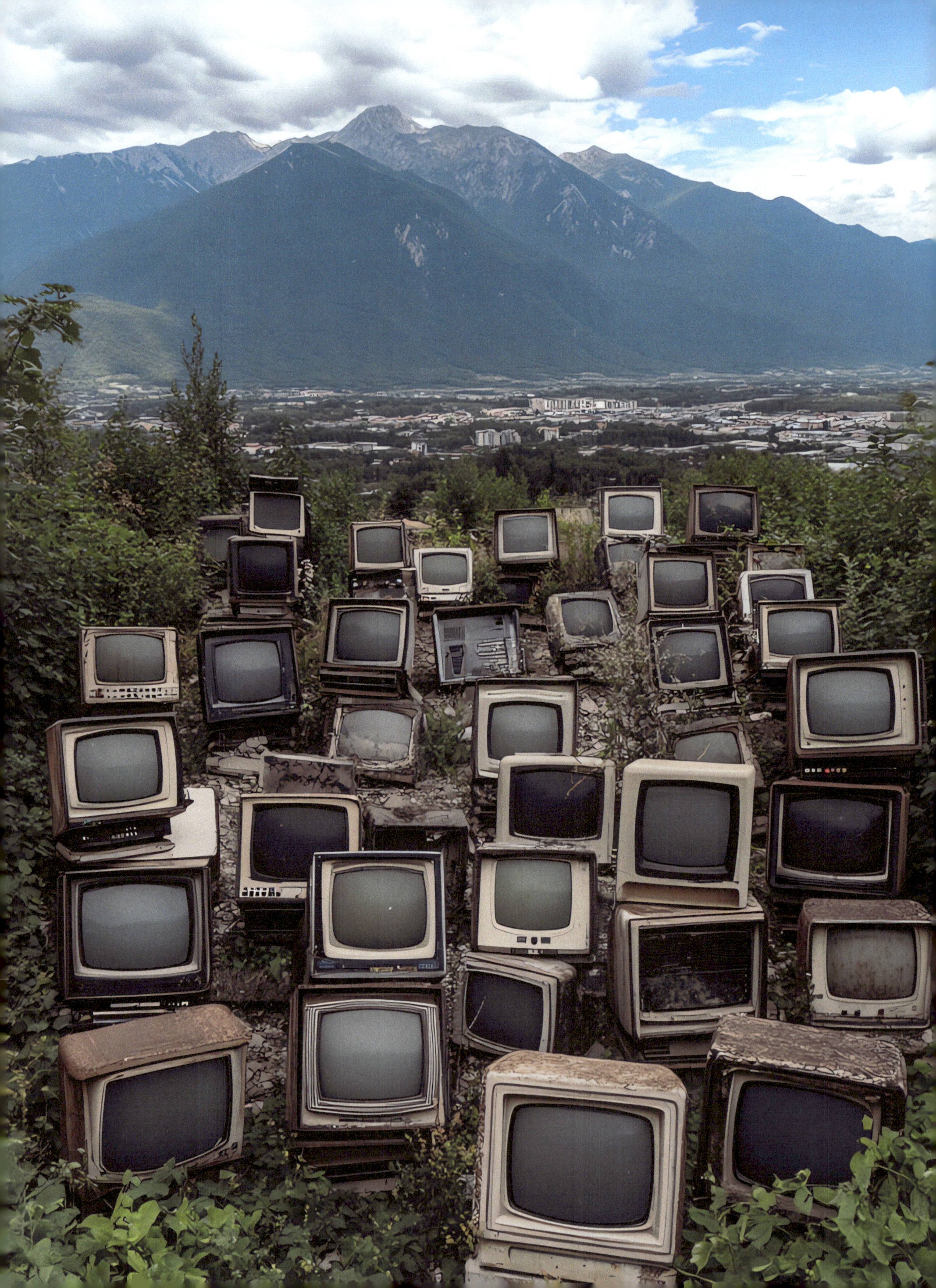

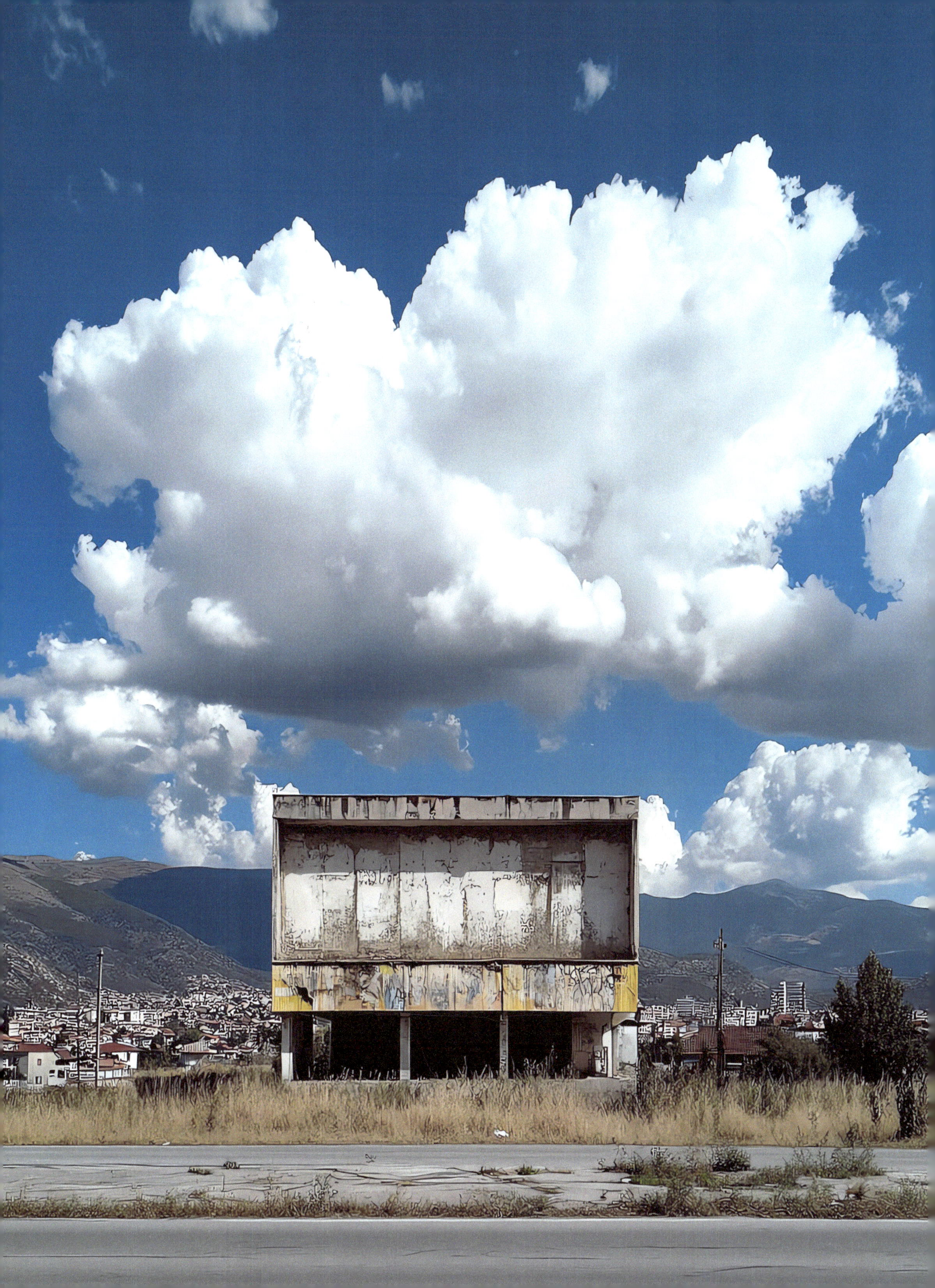

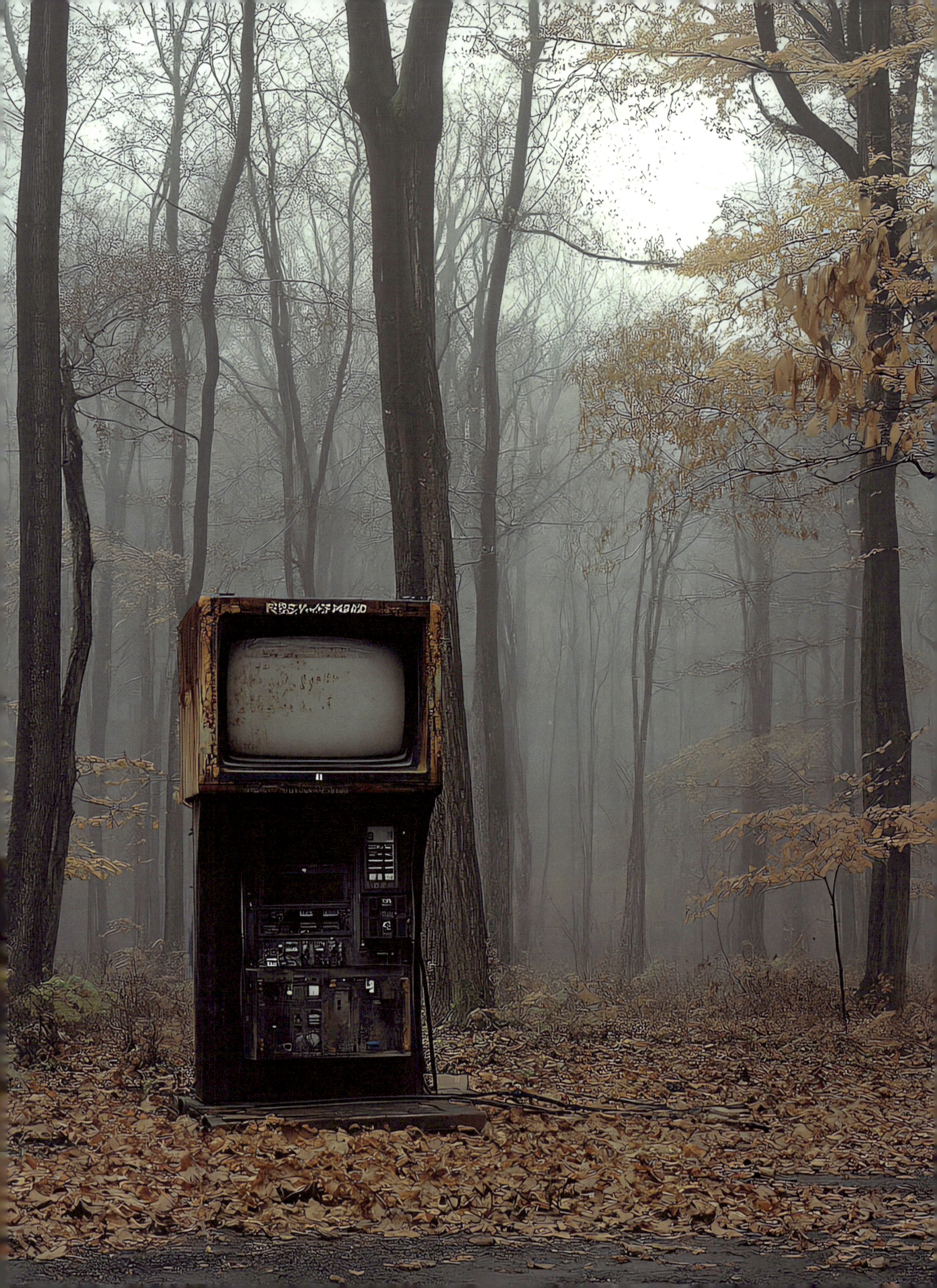

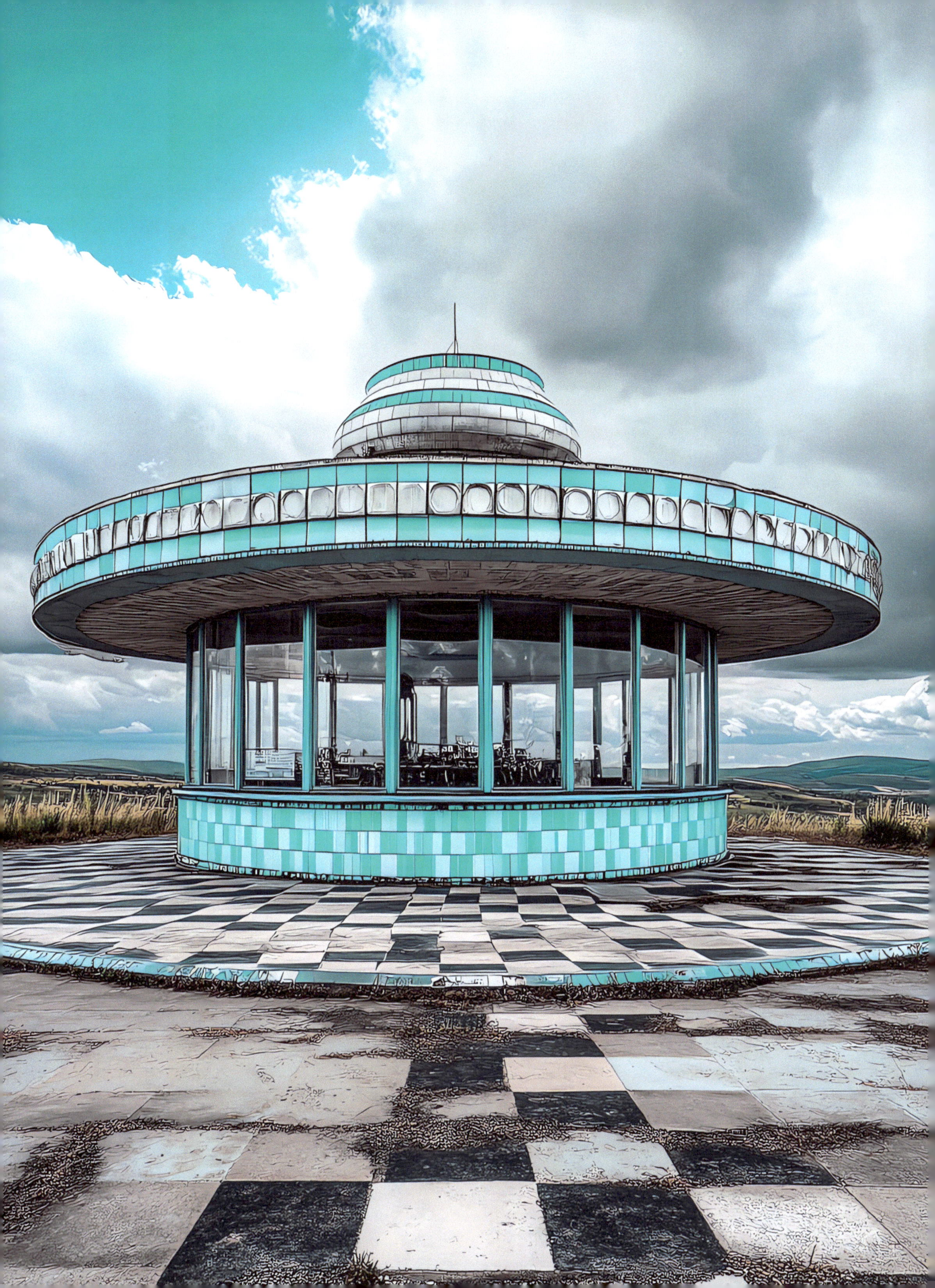

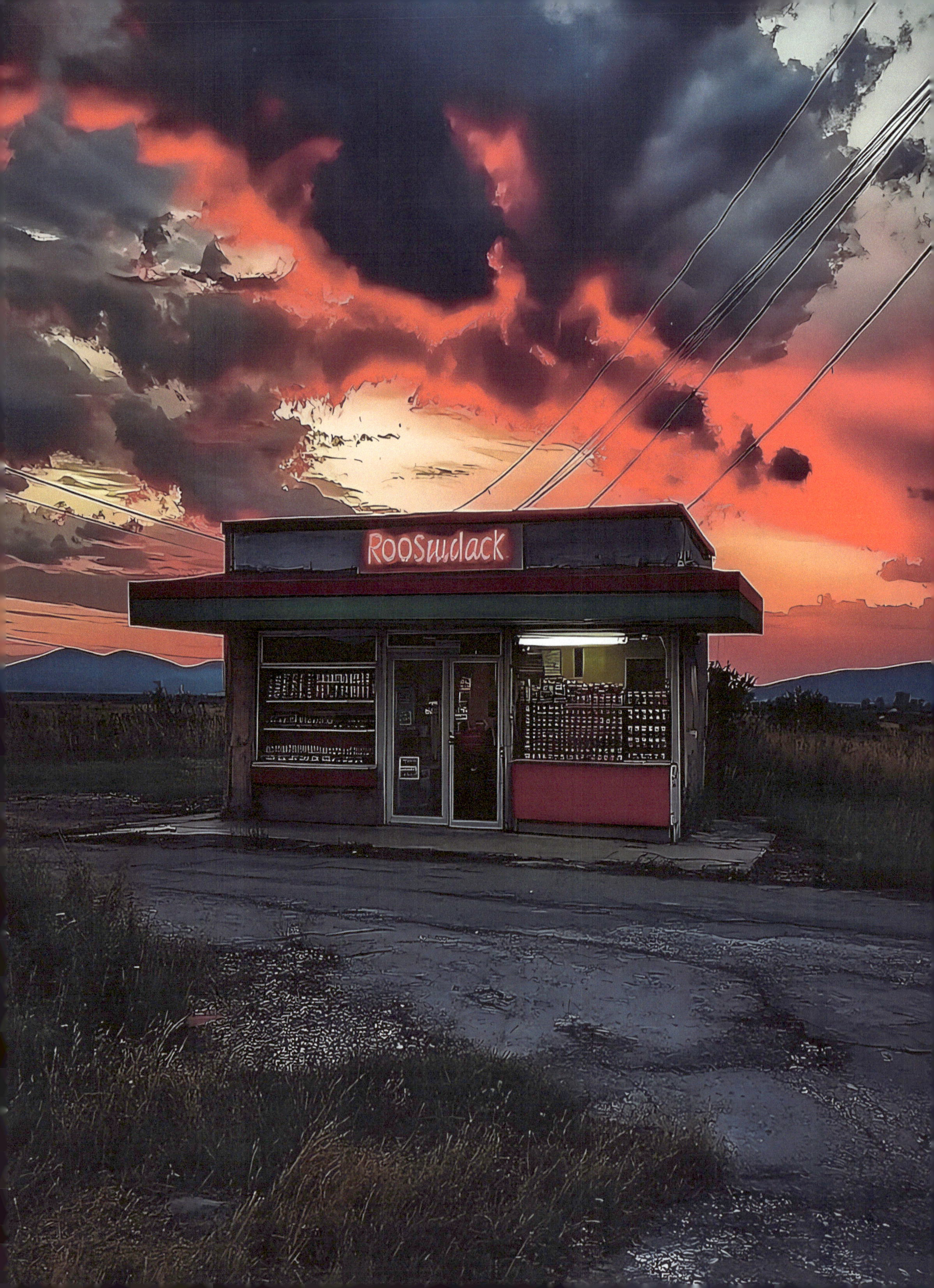
ROOSwdack

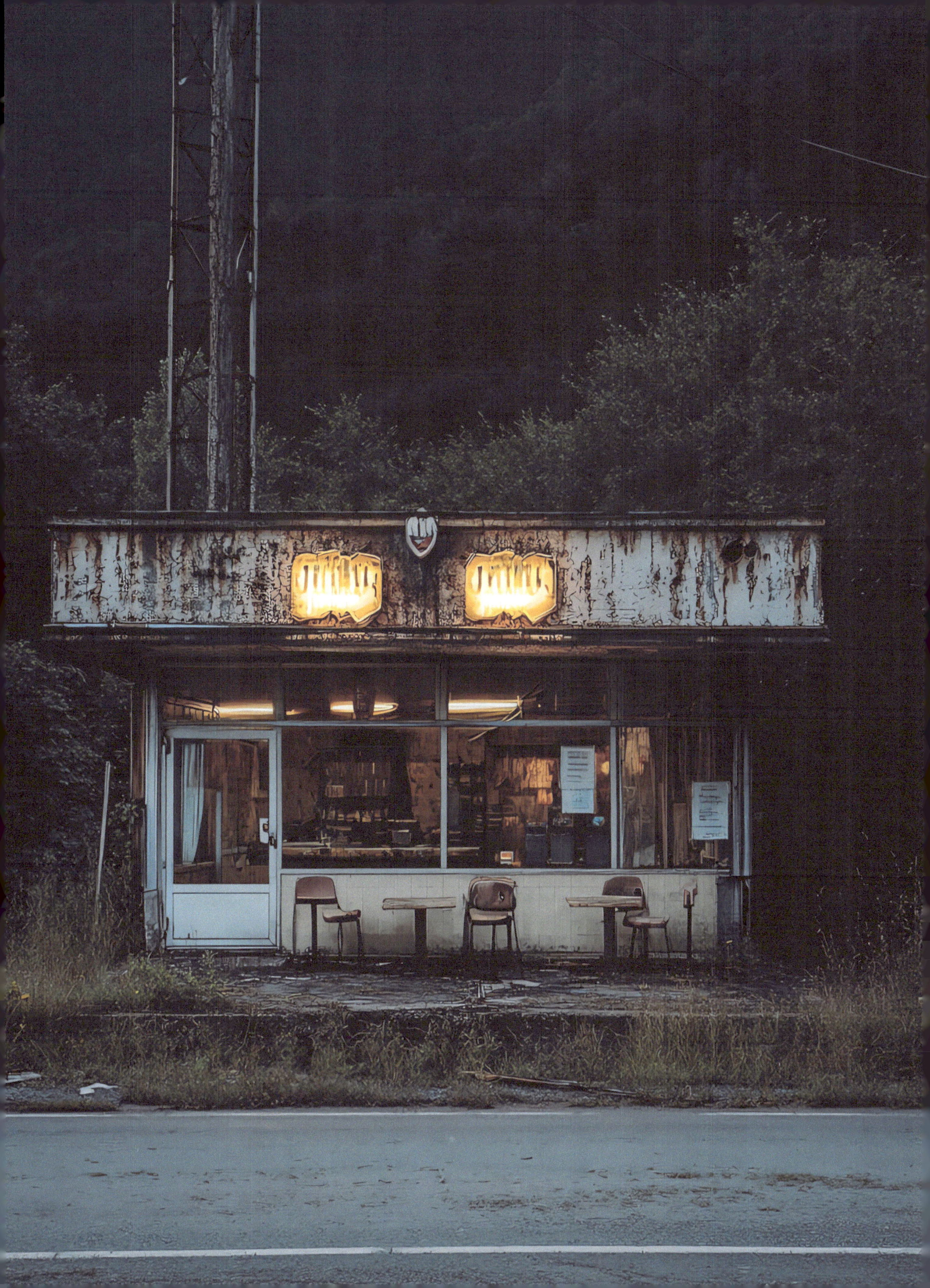

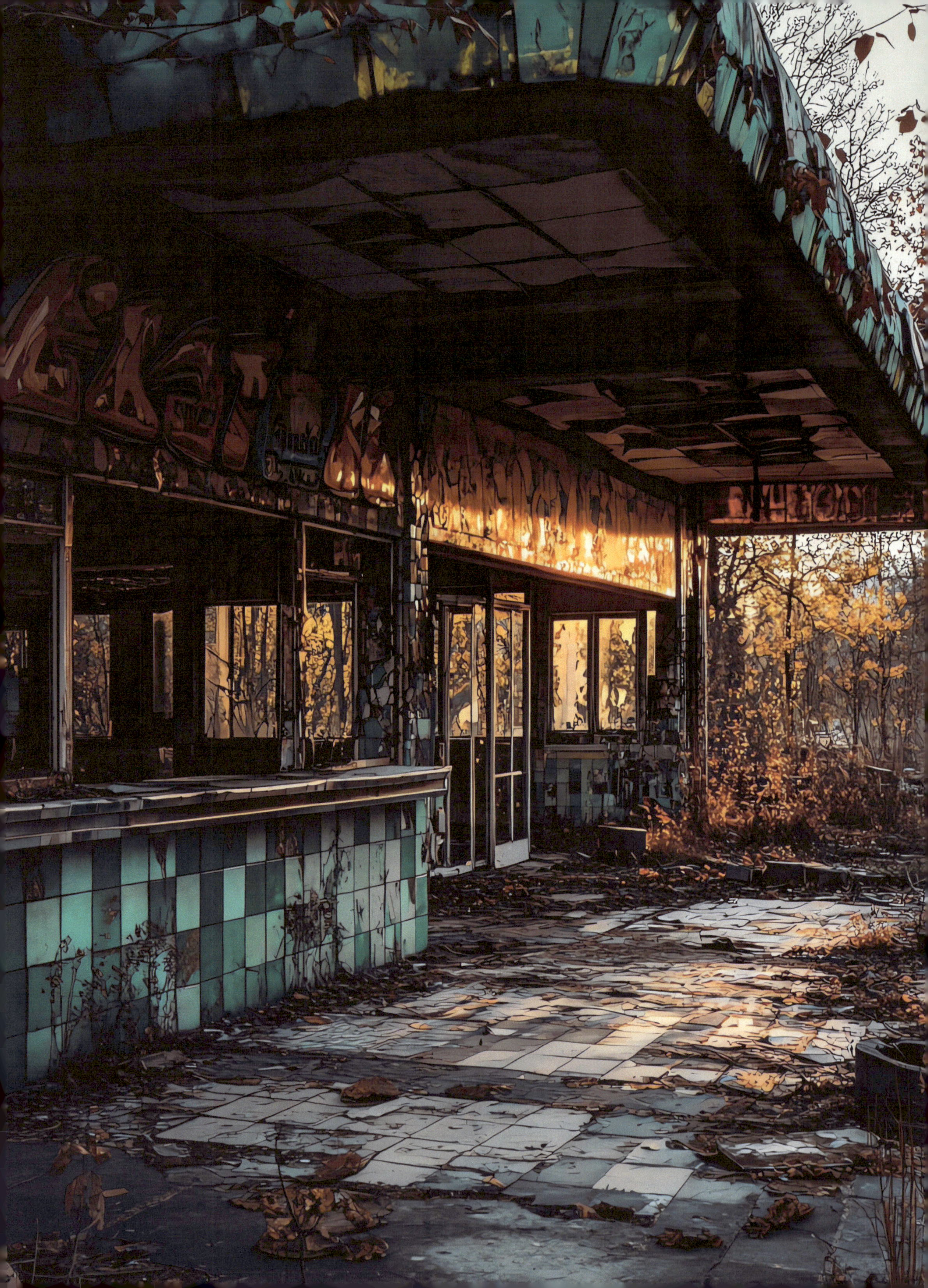

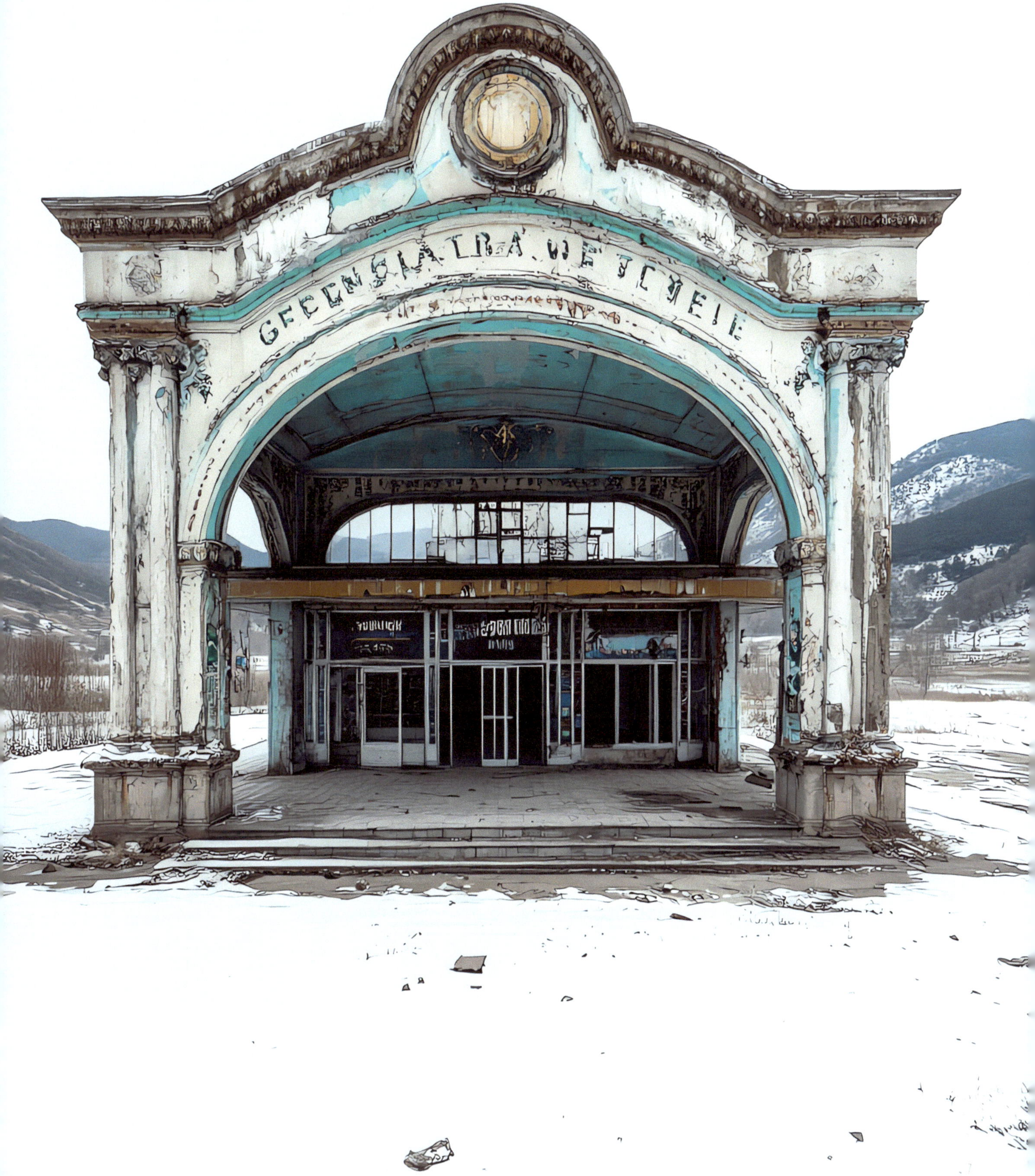

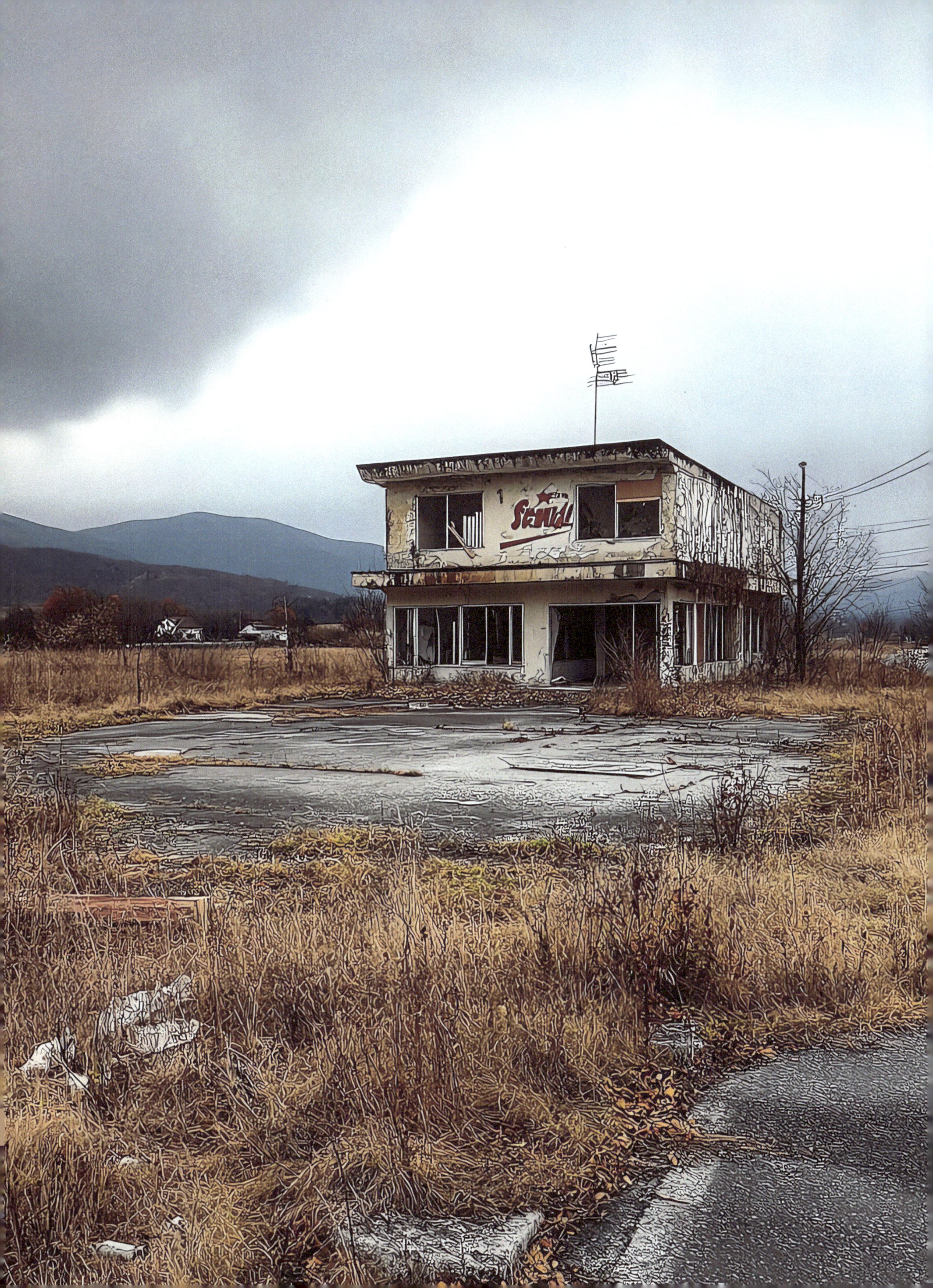

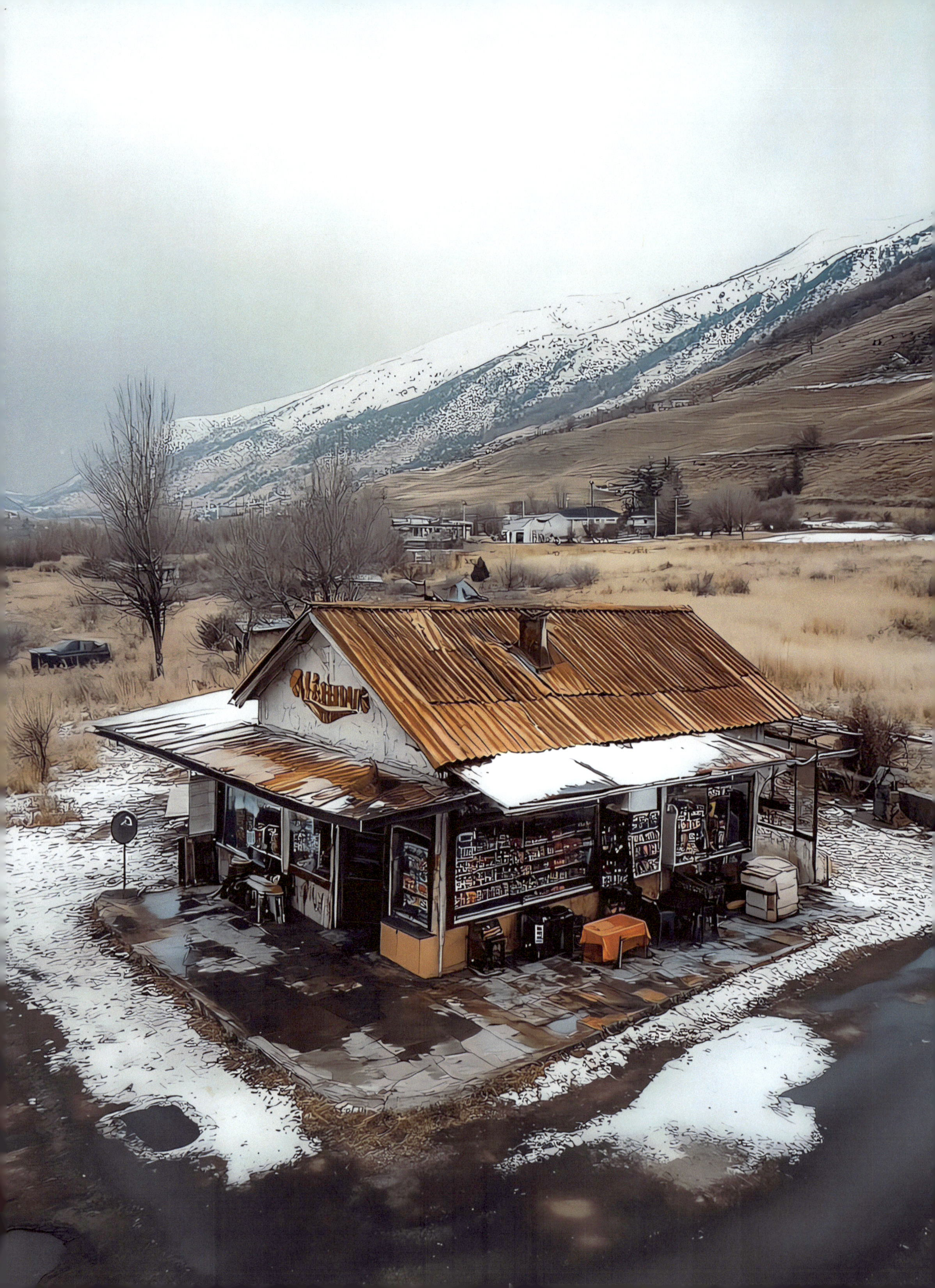

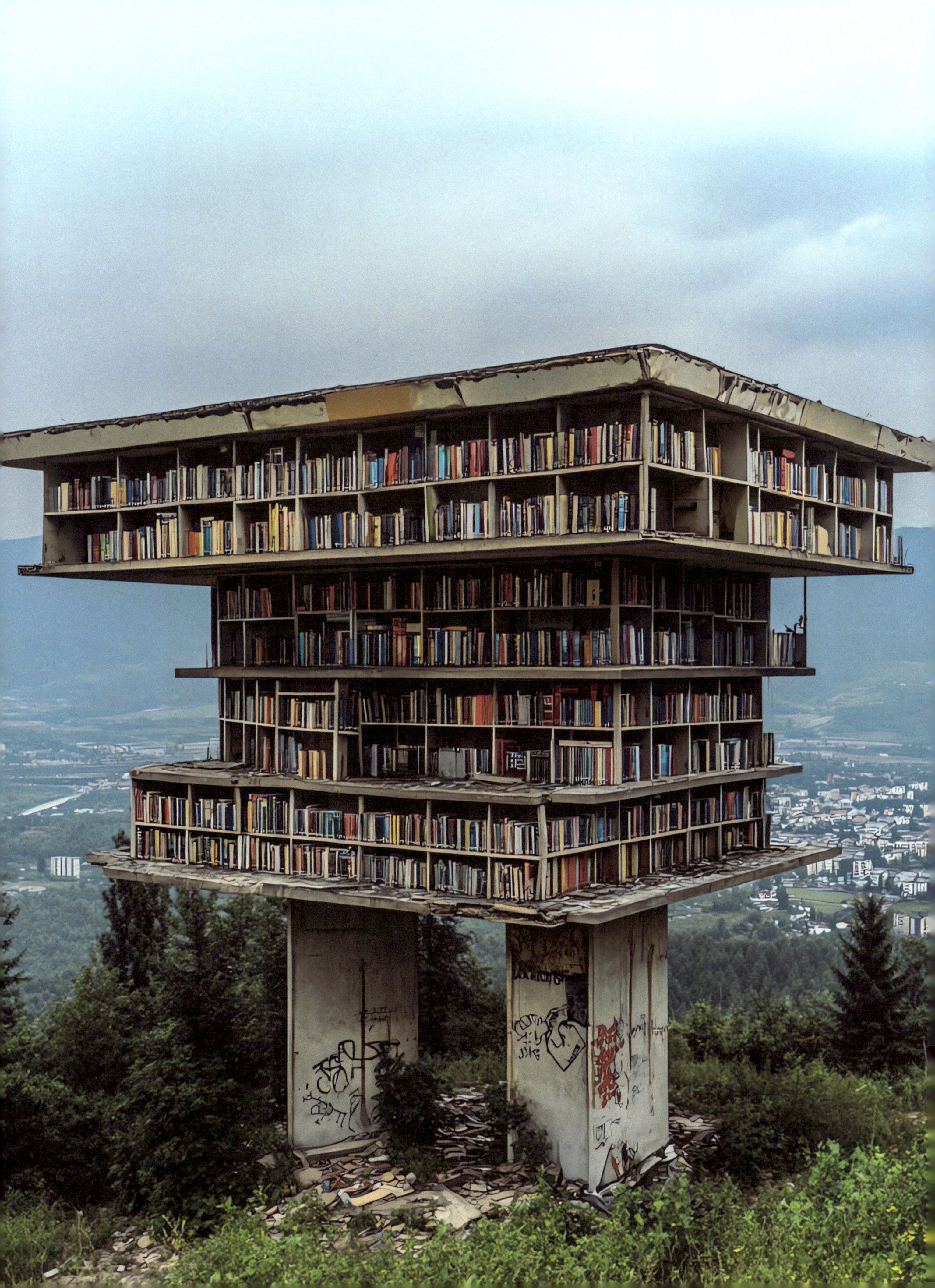

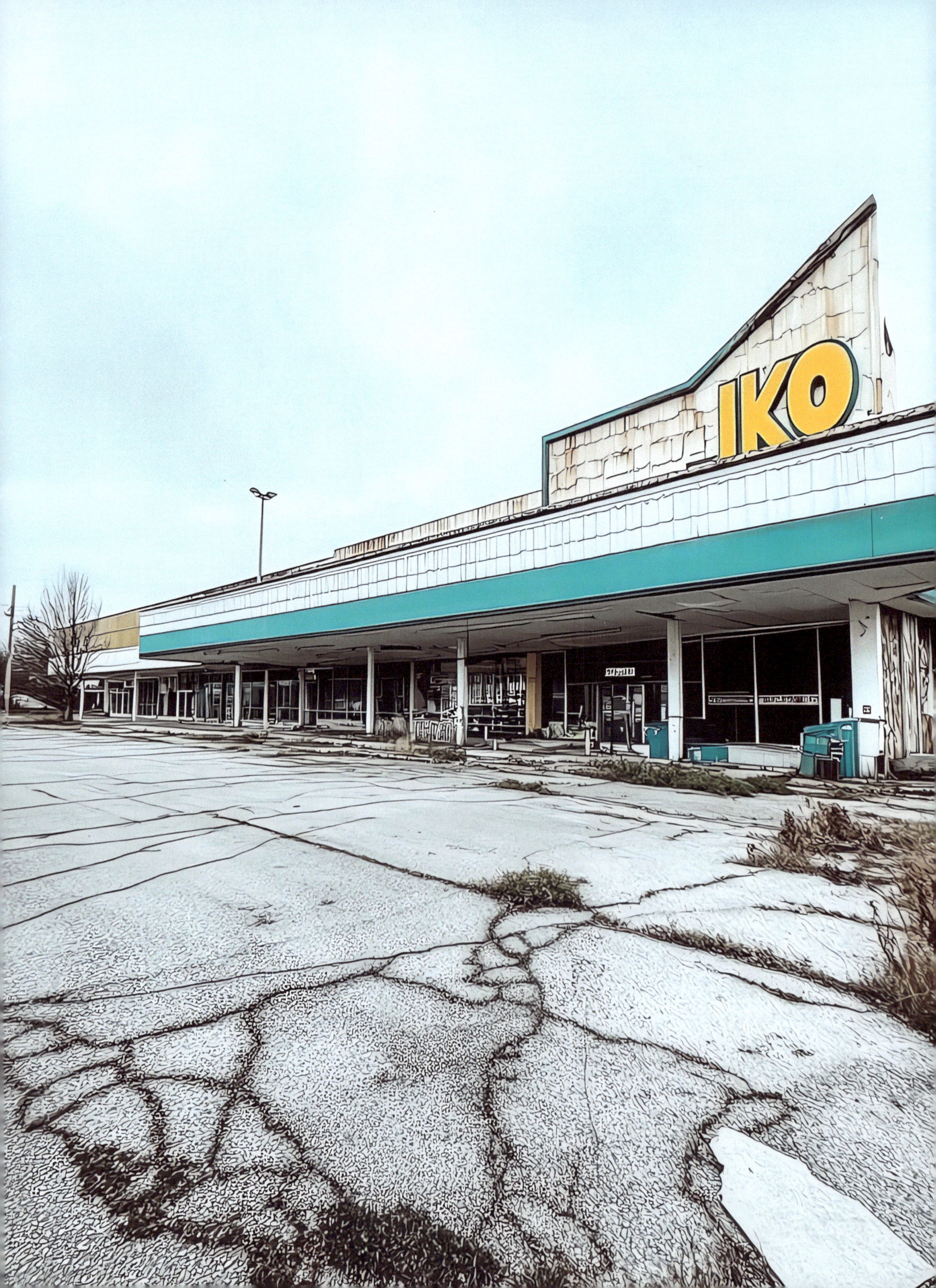
IKO

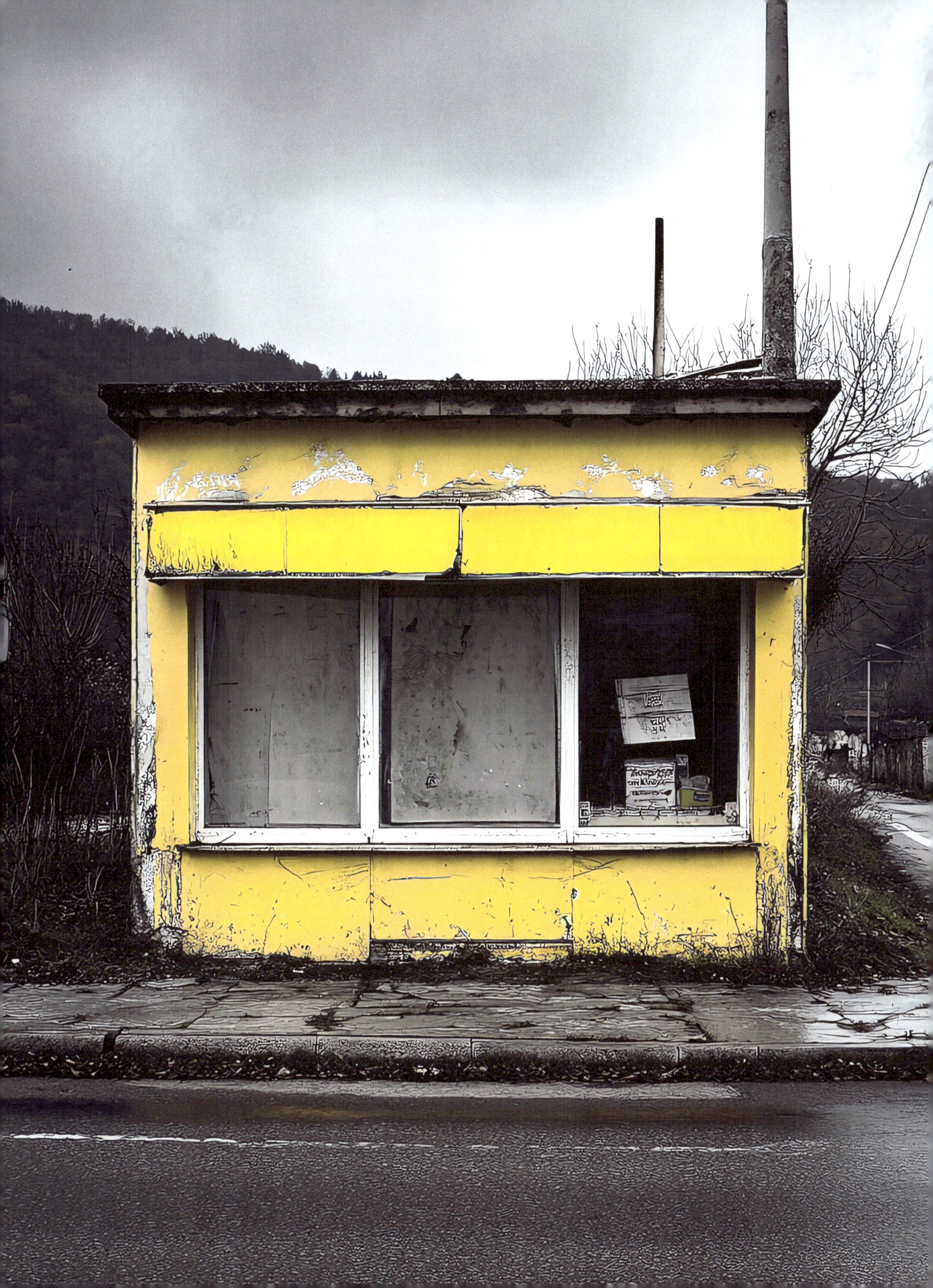

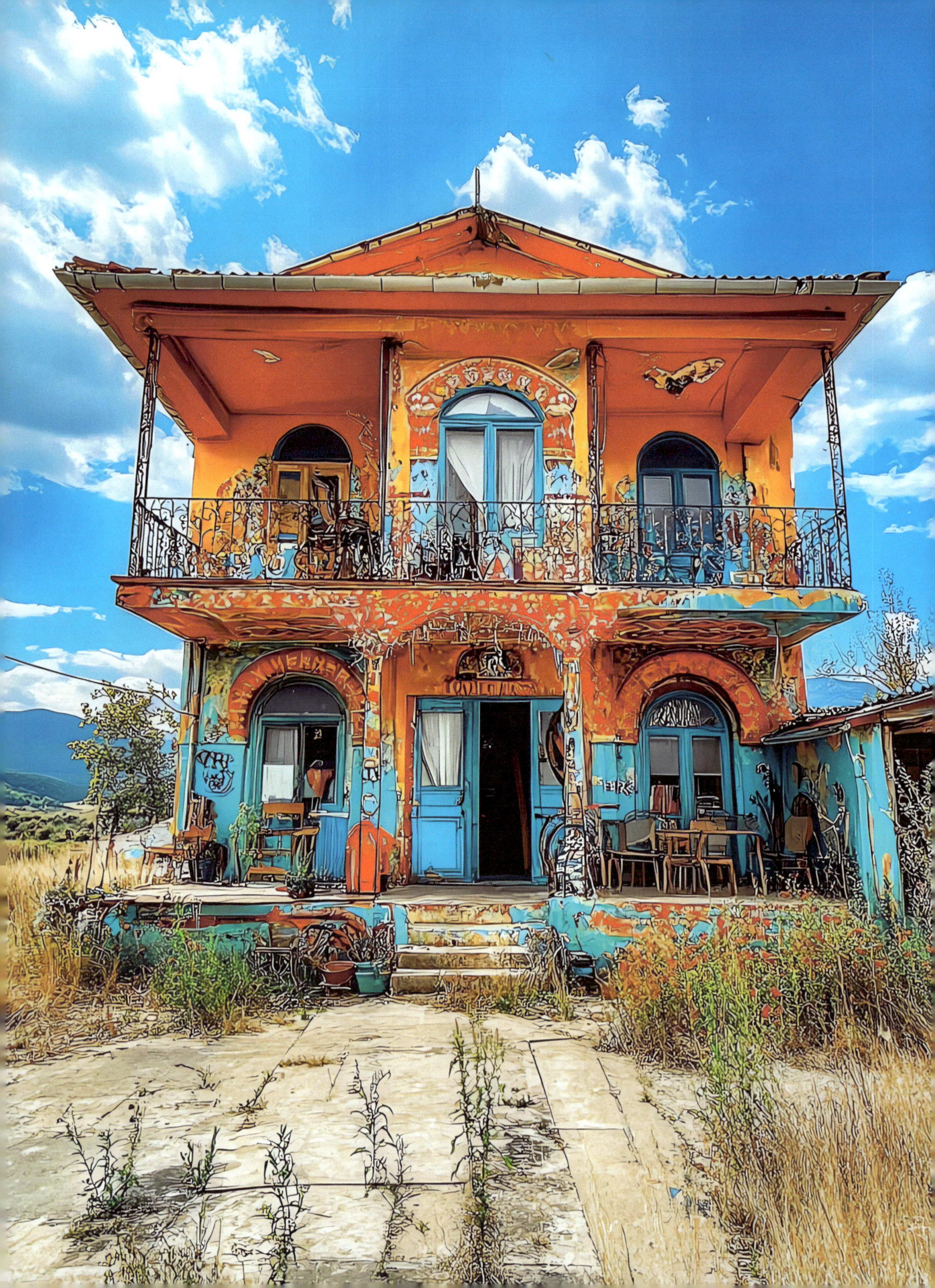

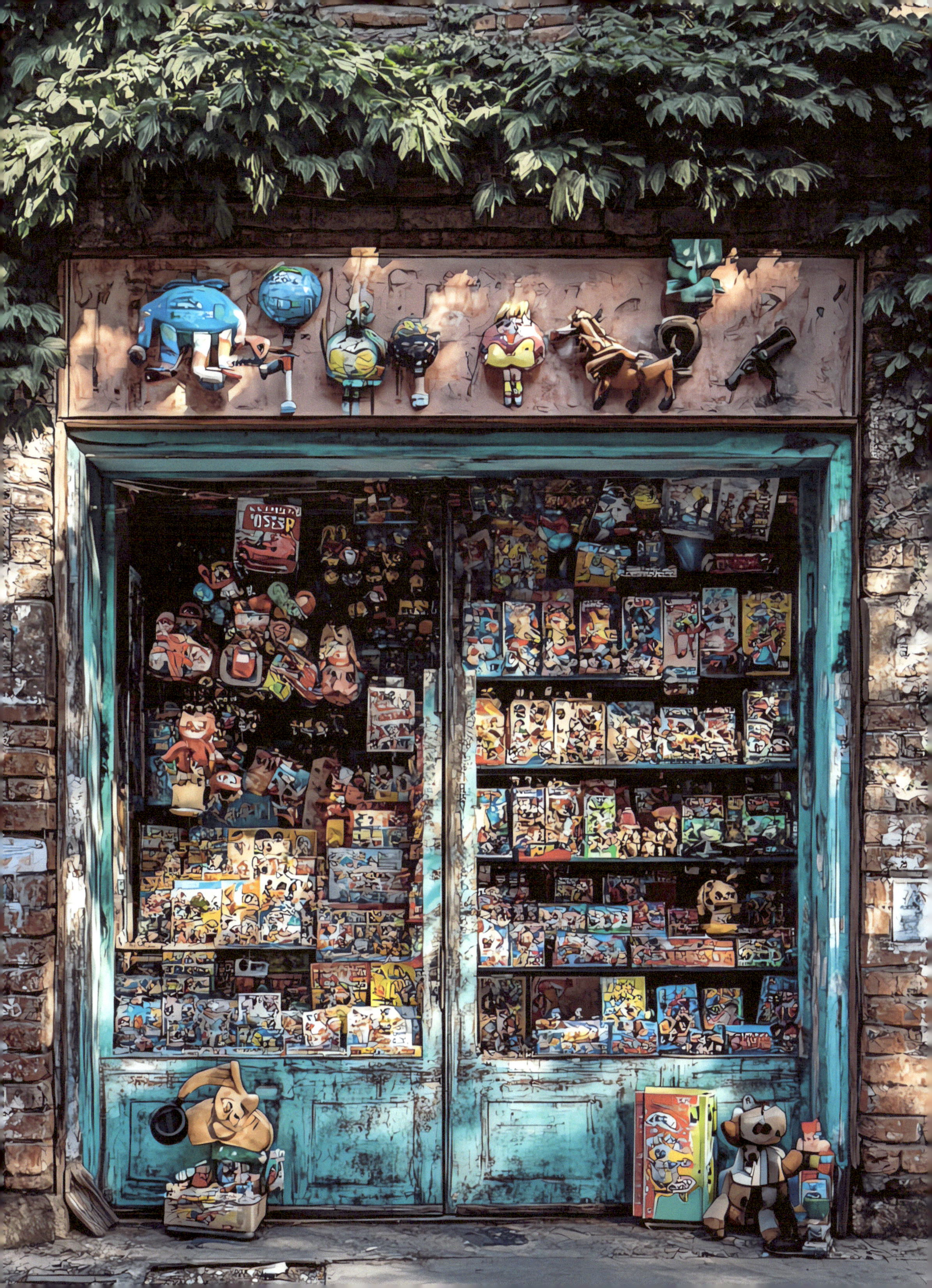

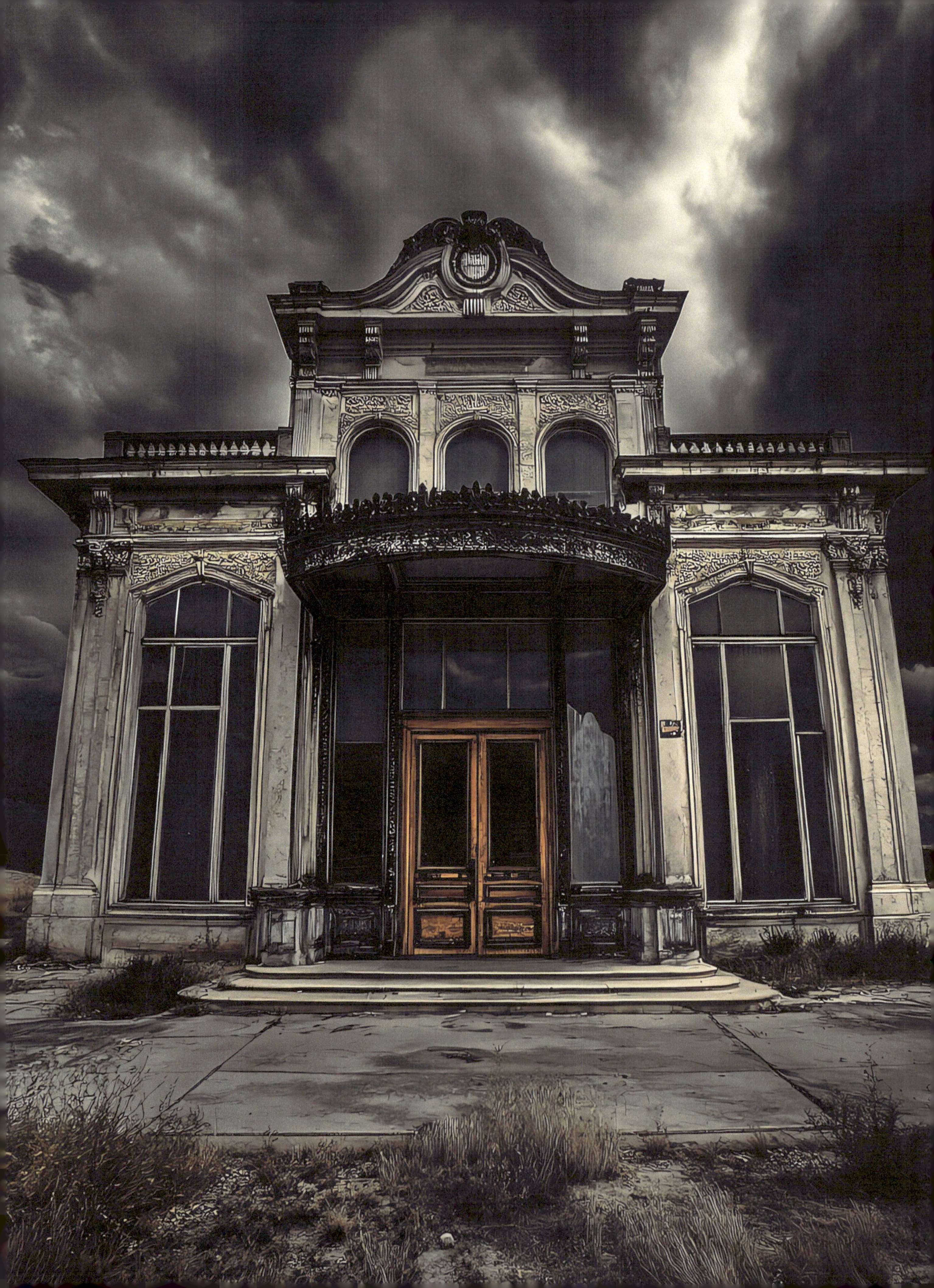

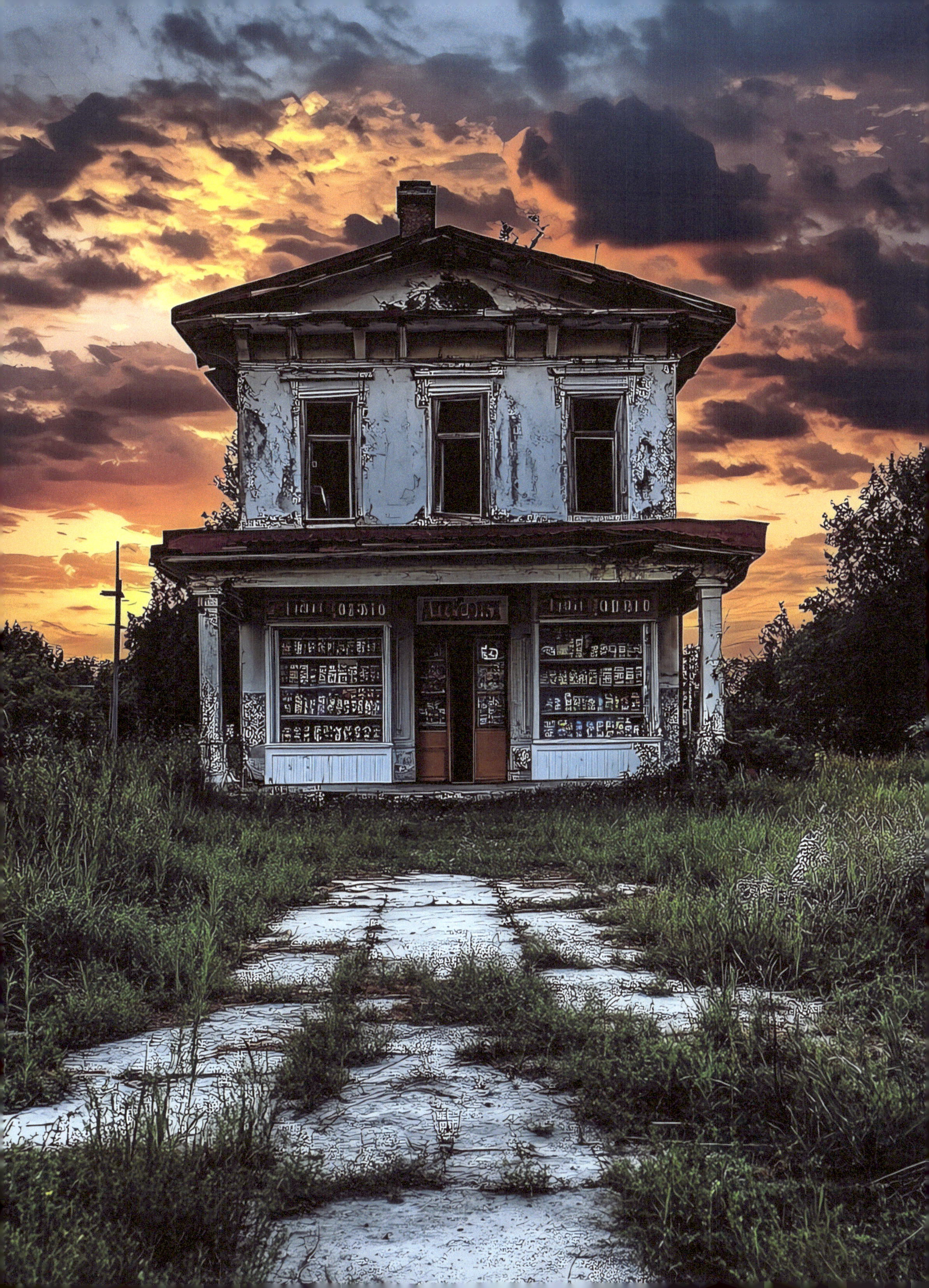

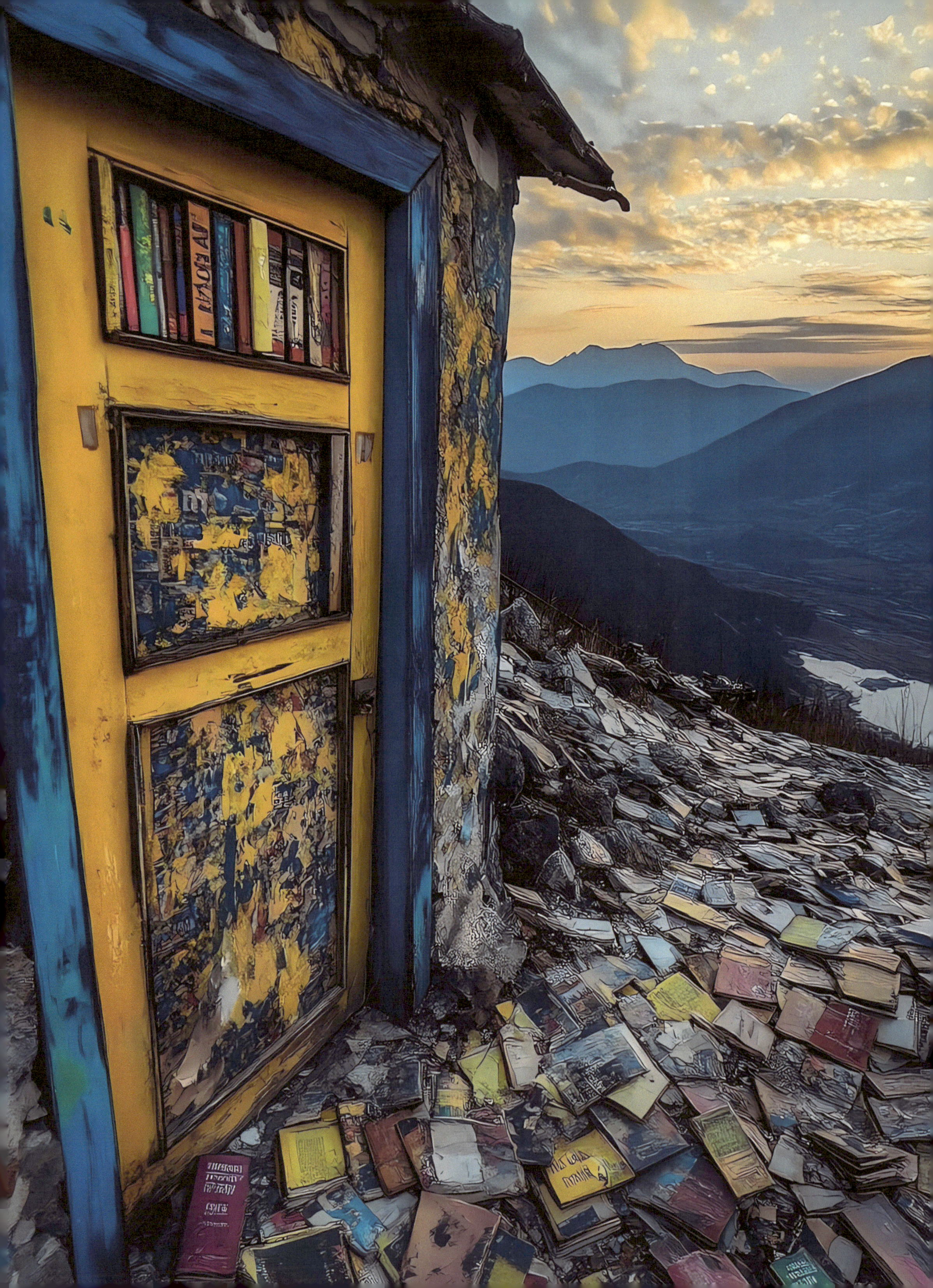

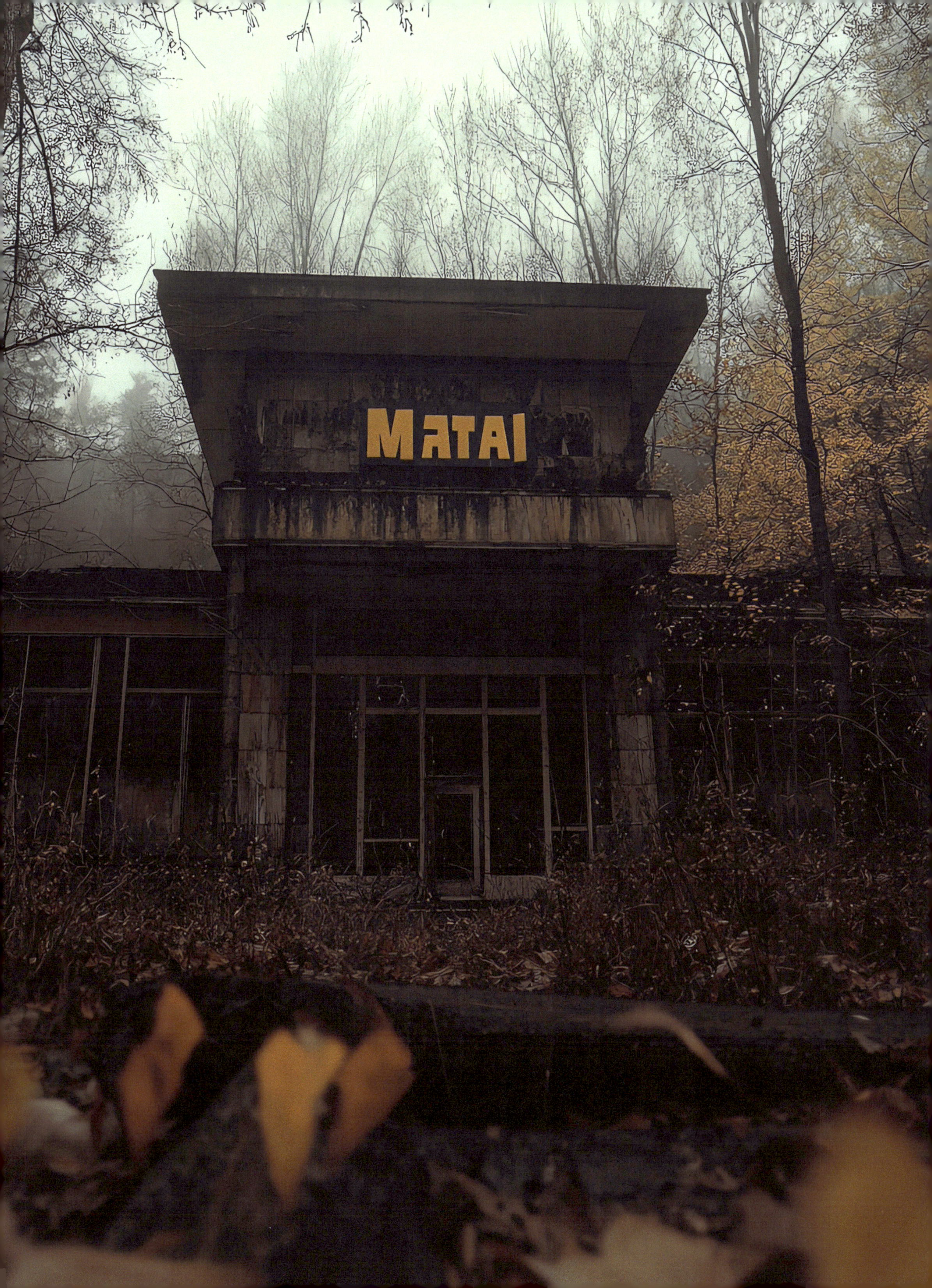
MATAI

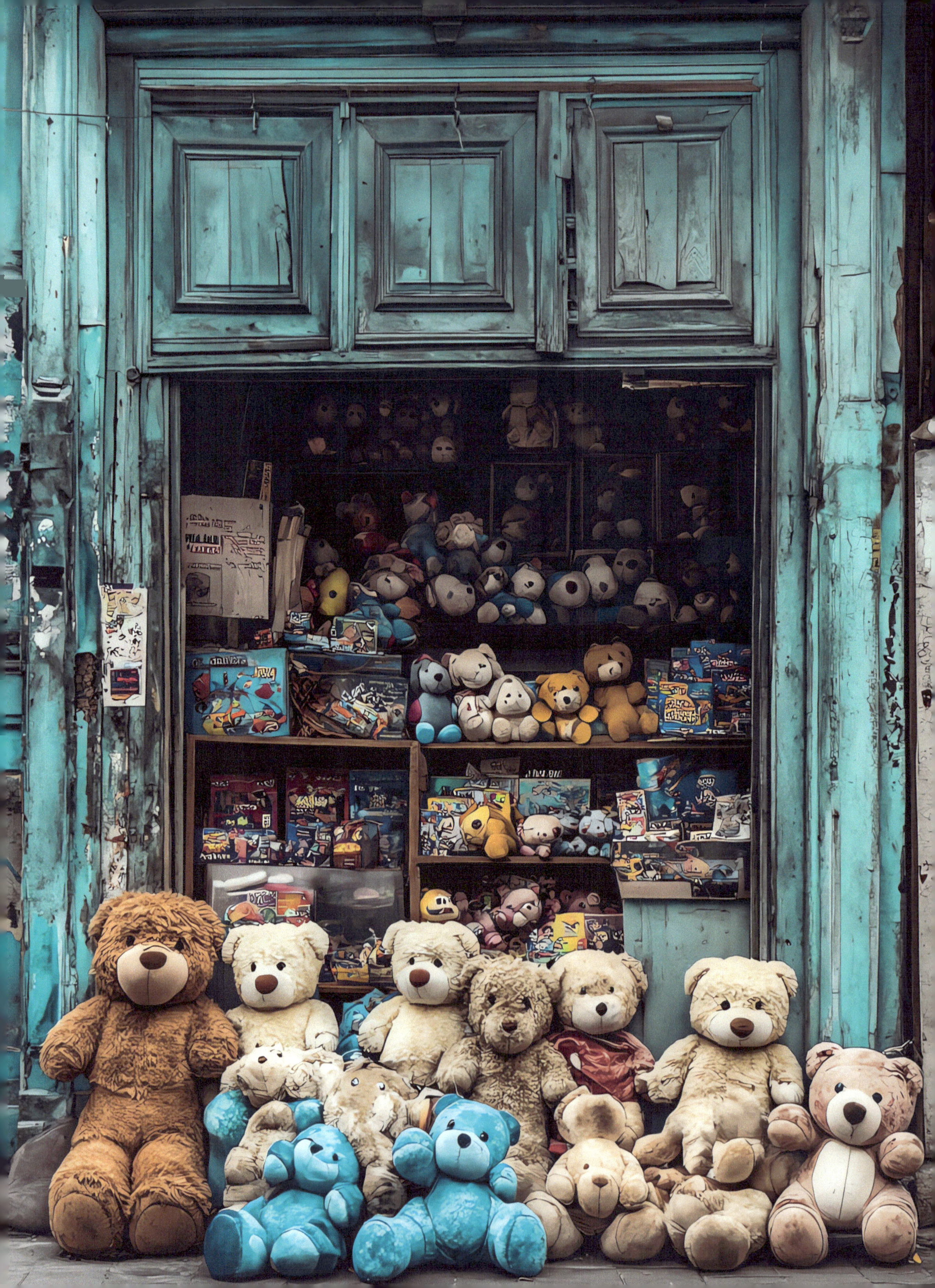

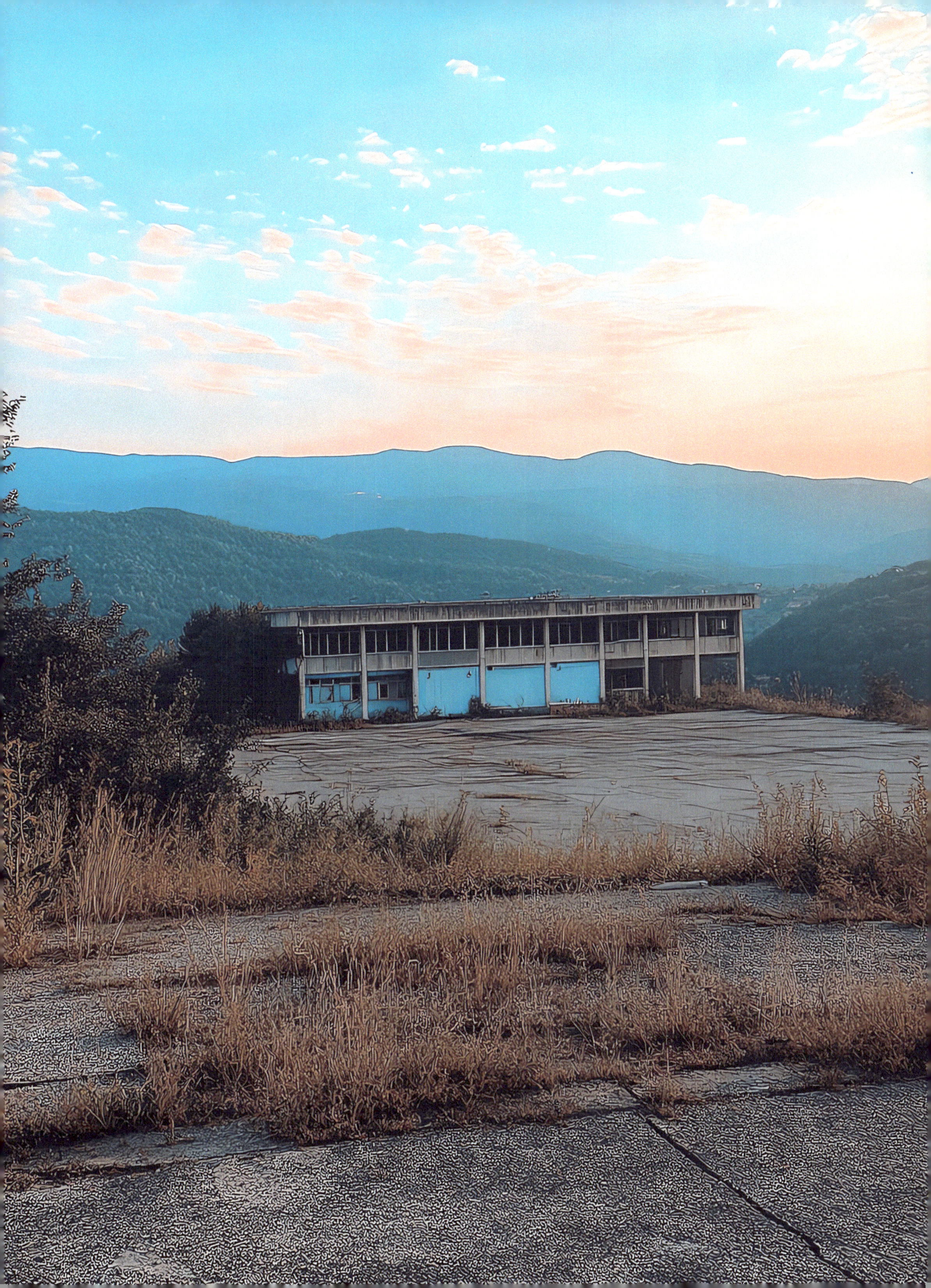

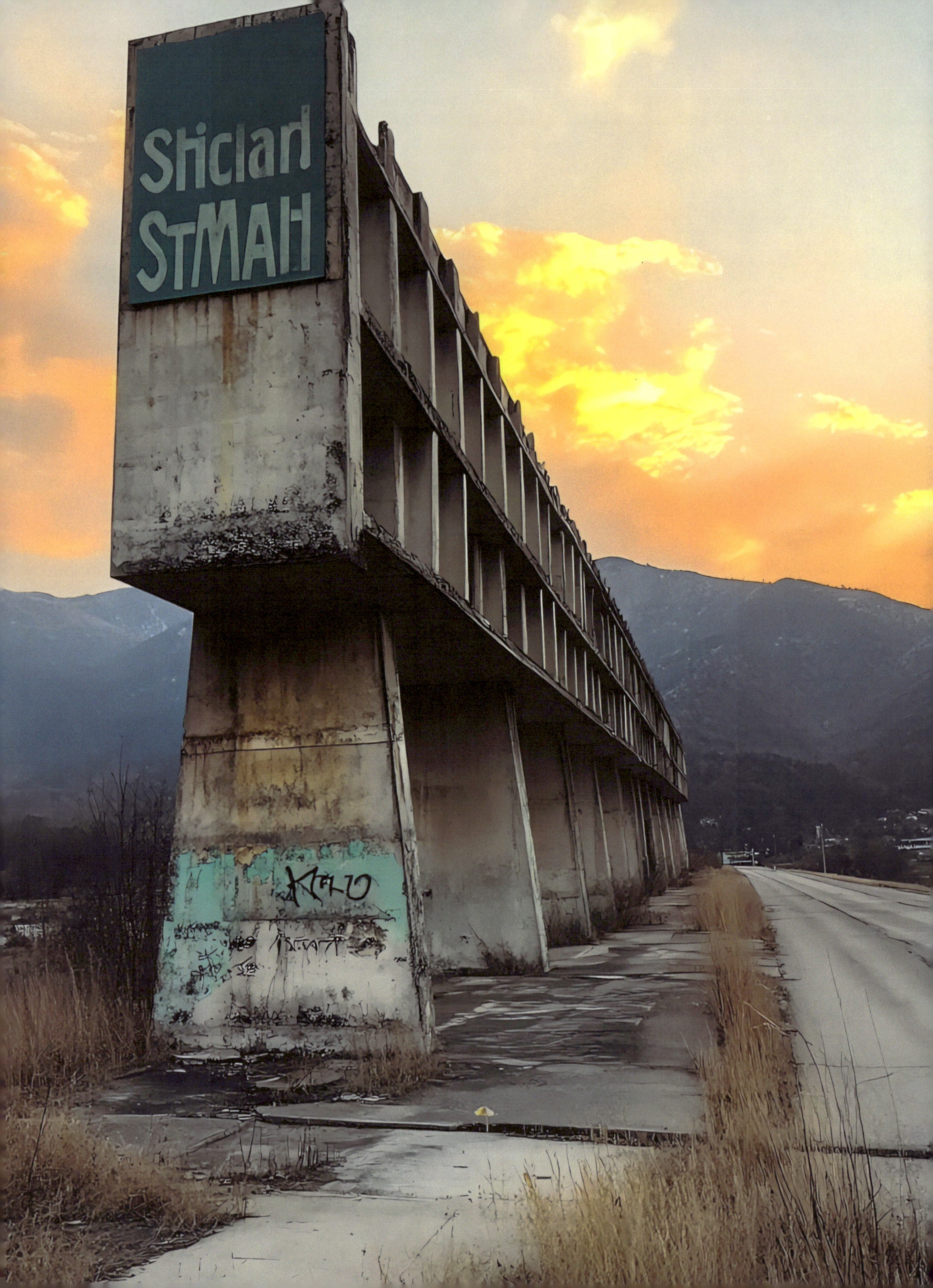
Shiclarl
StMAH

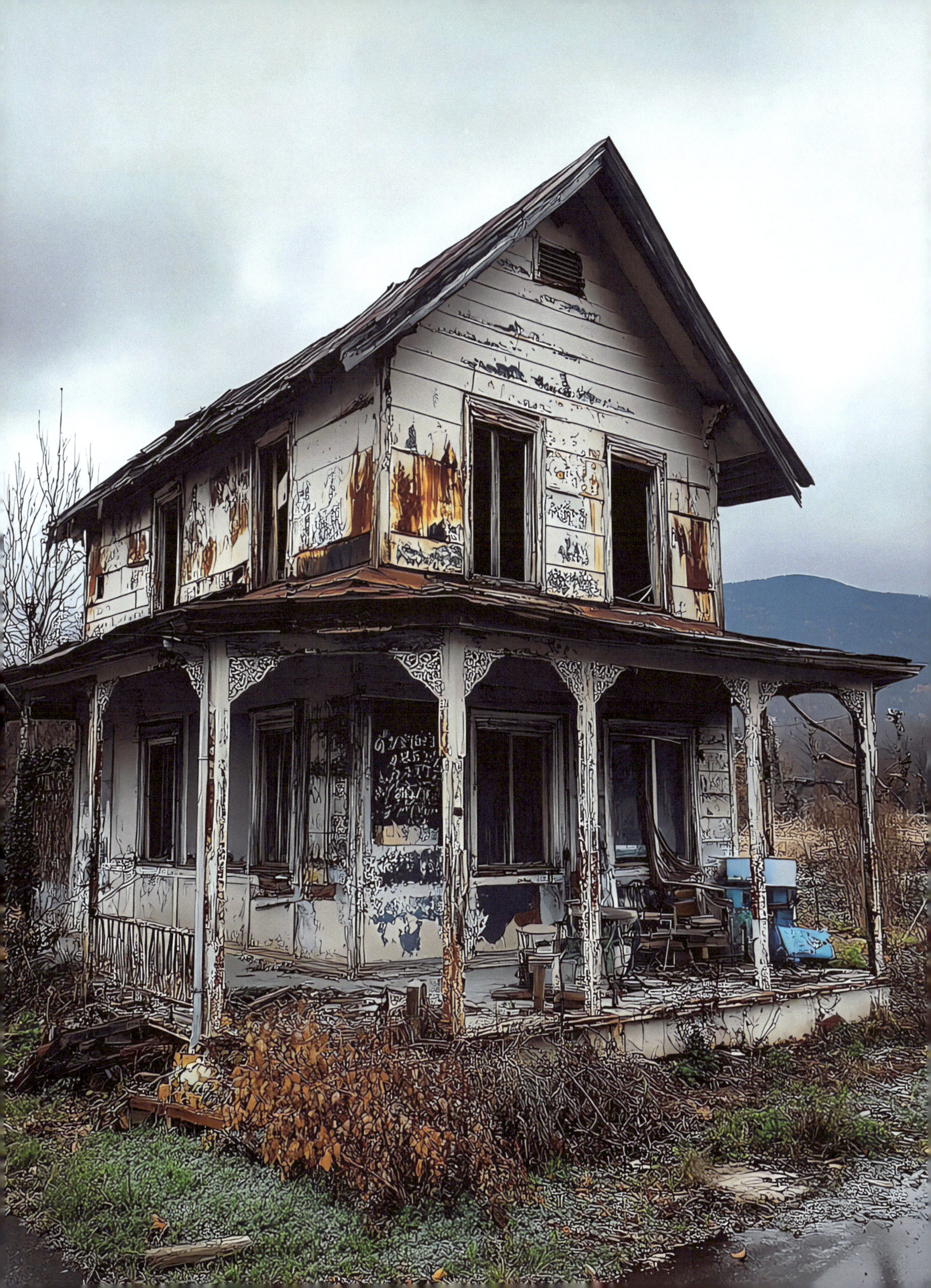

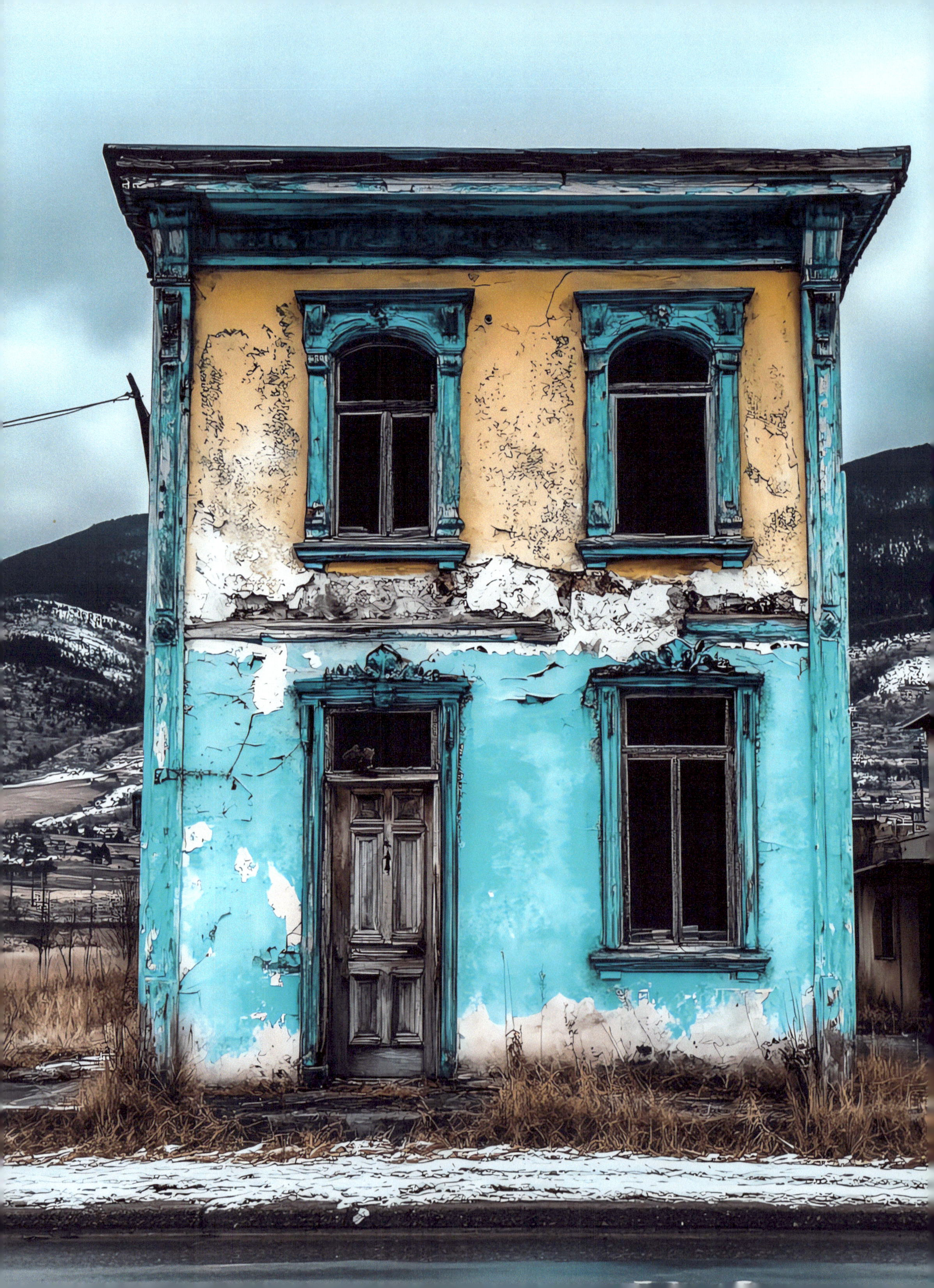

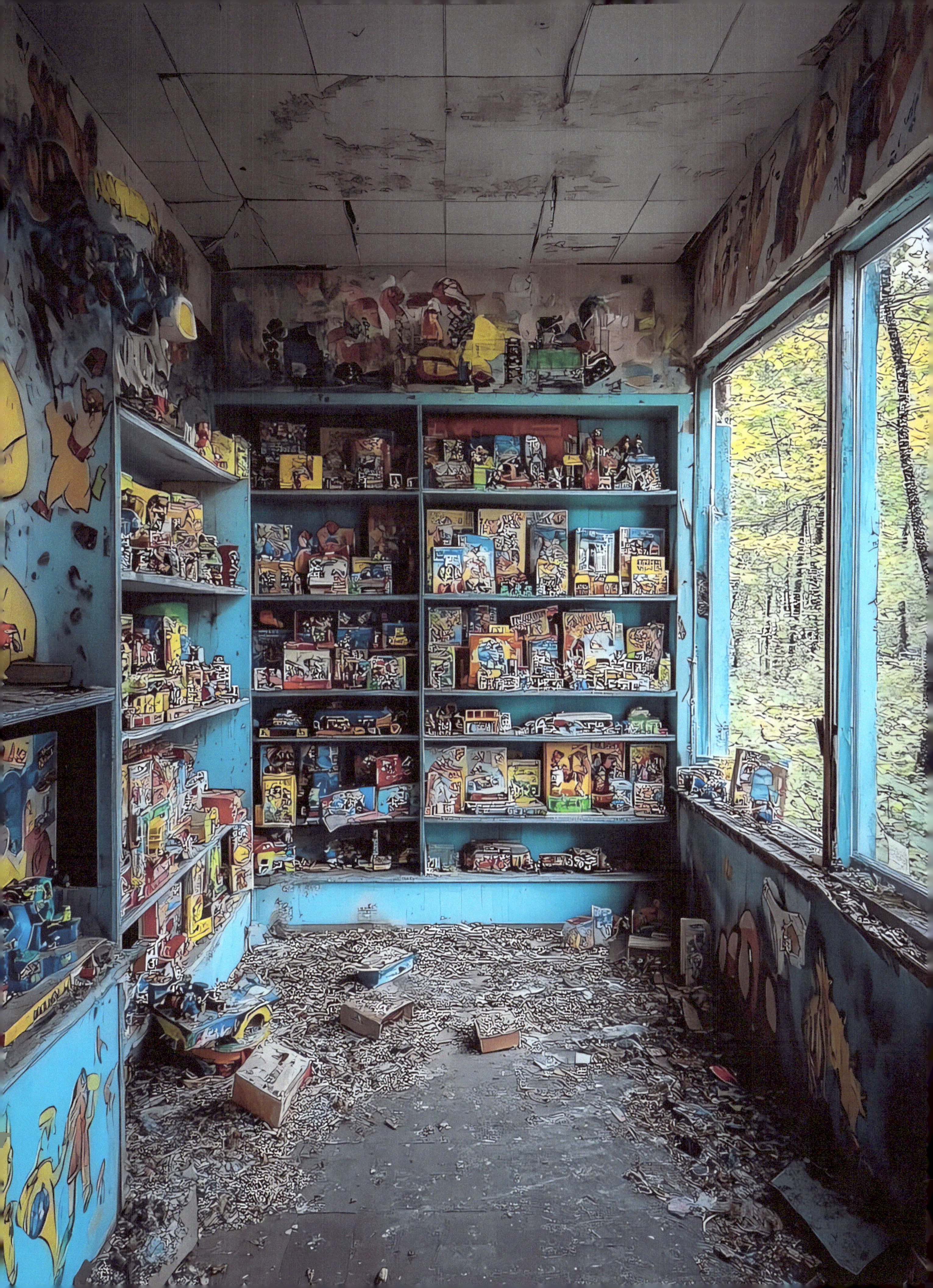

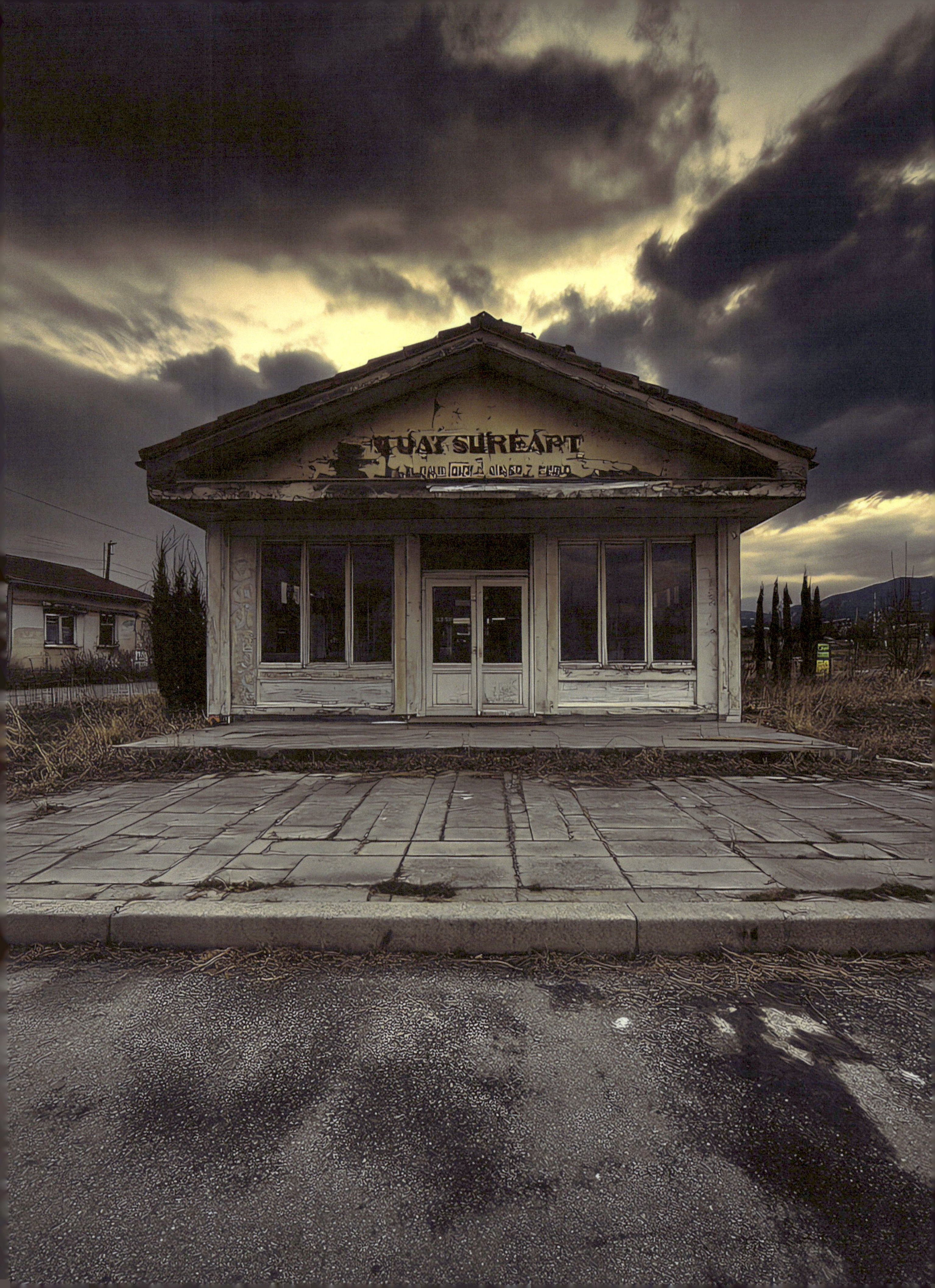

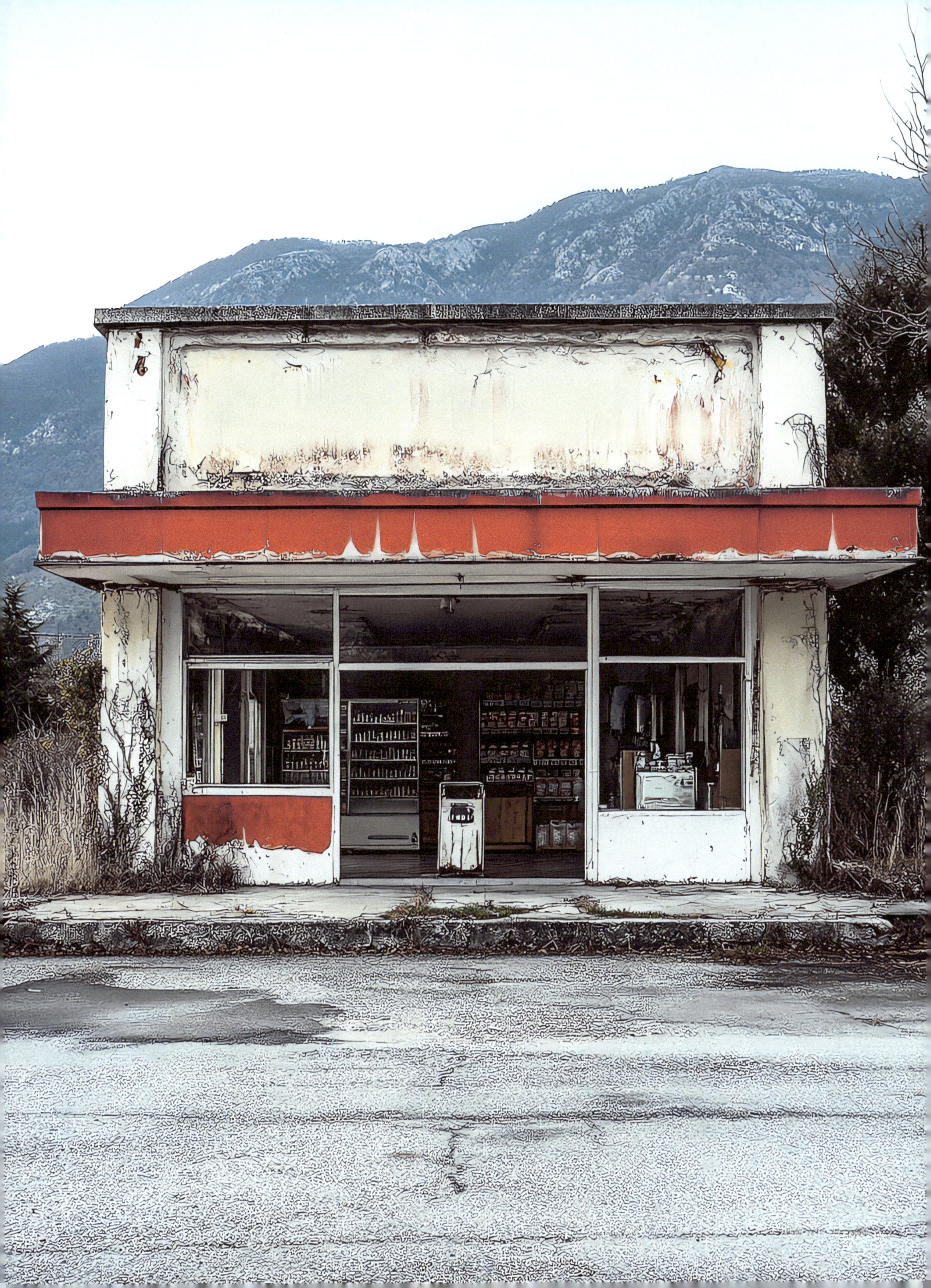

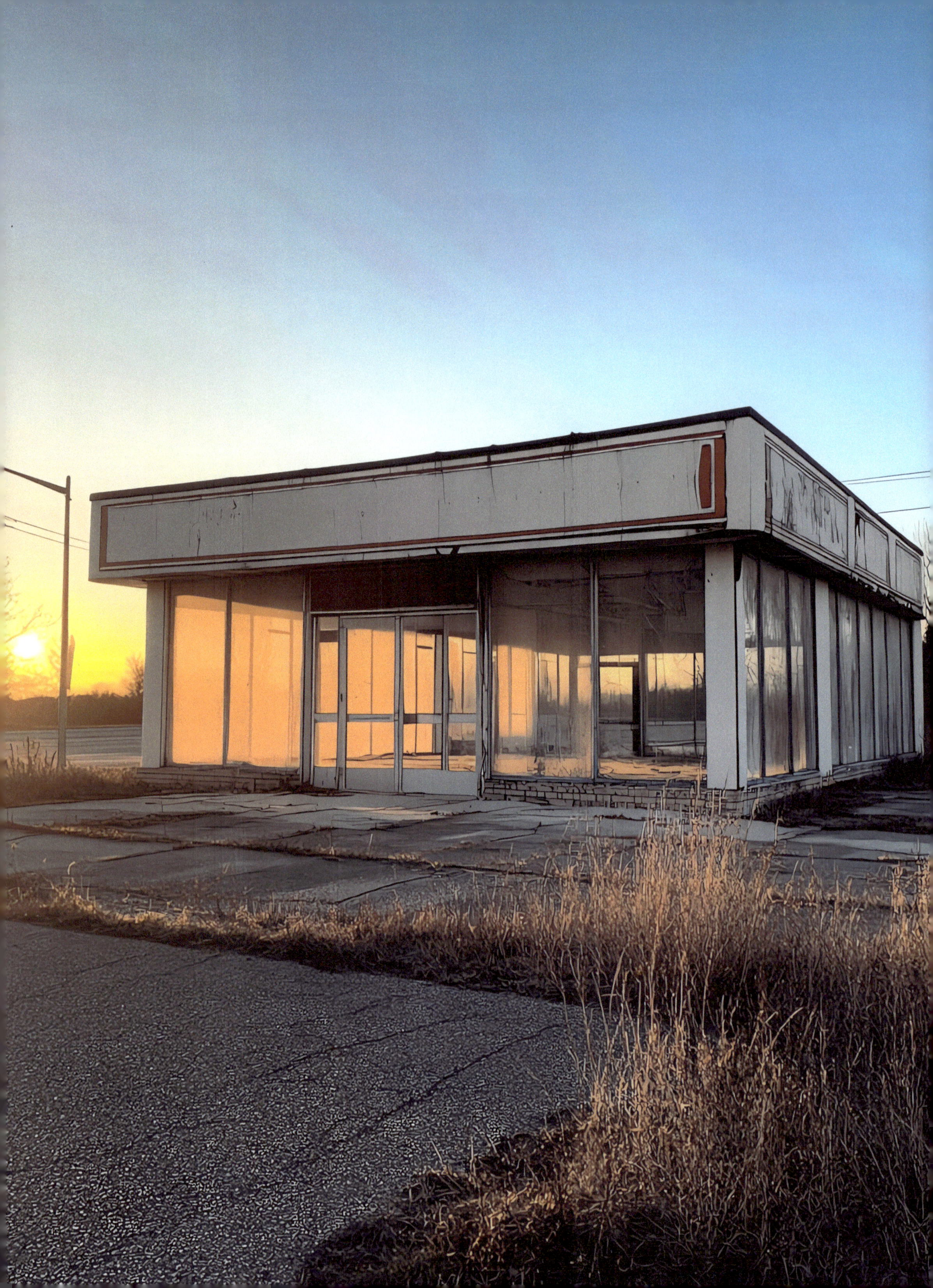

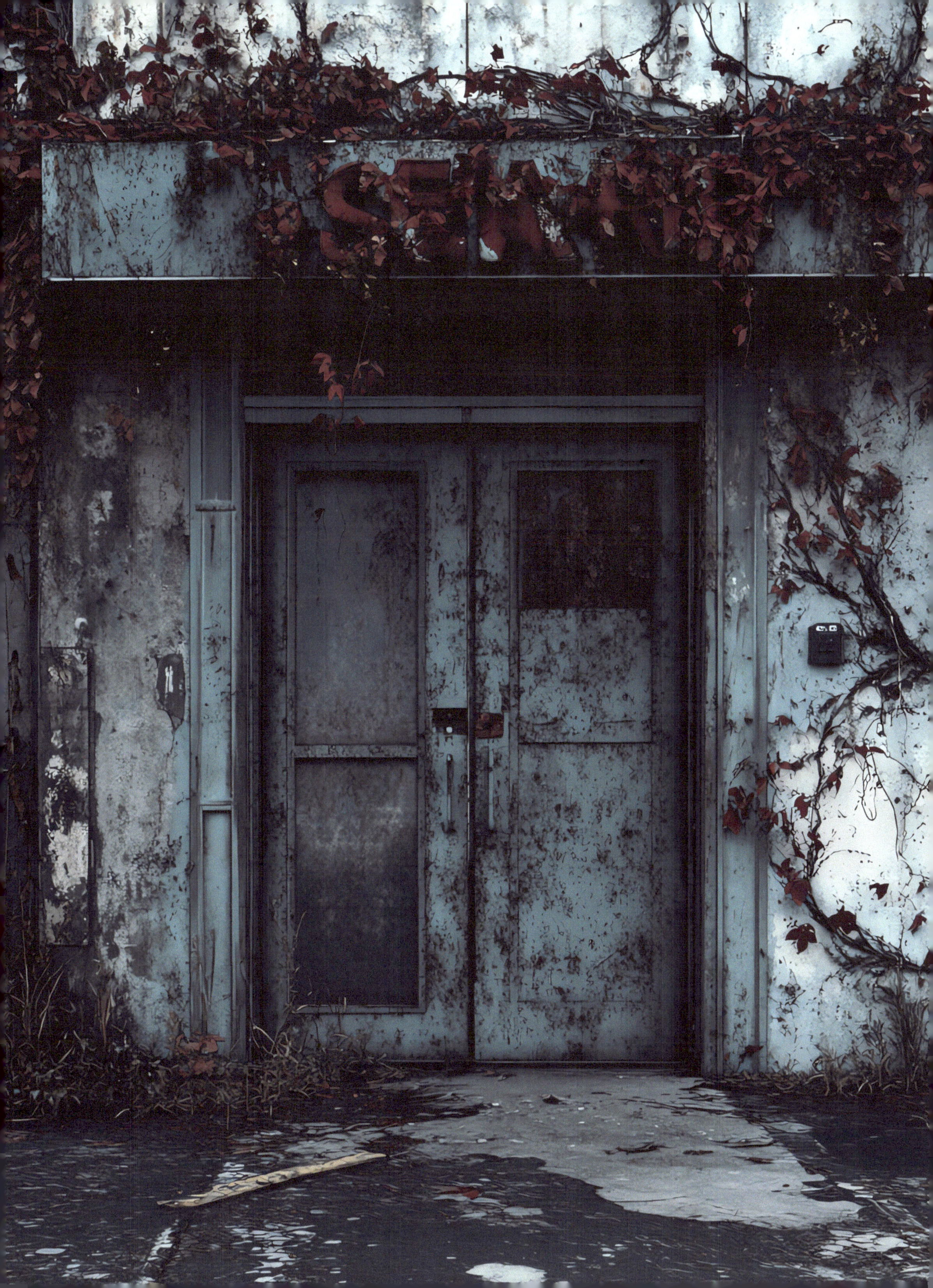

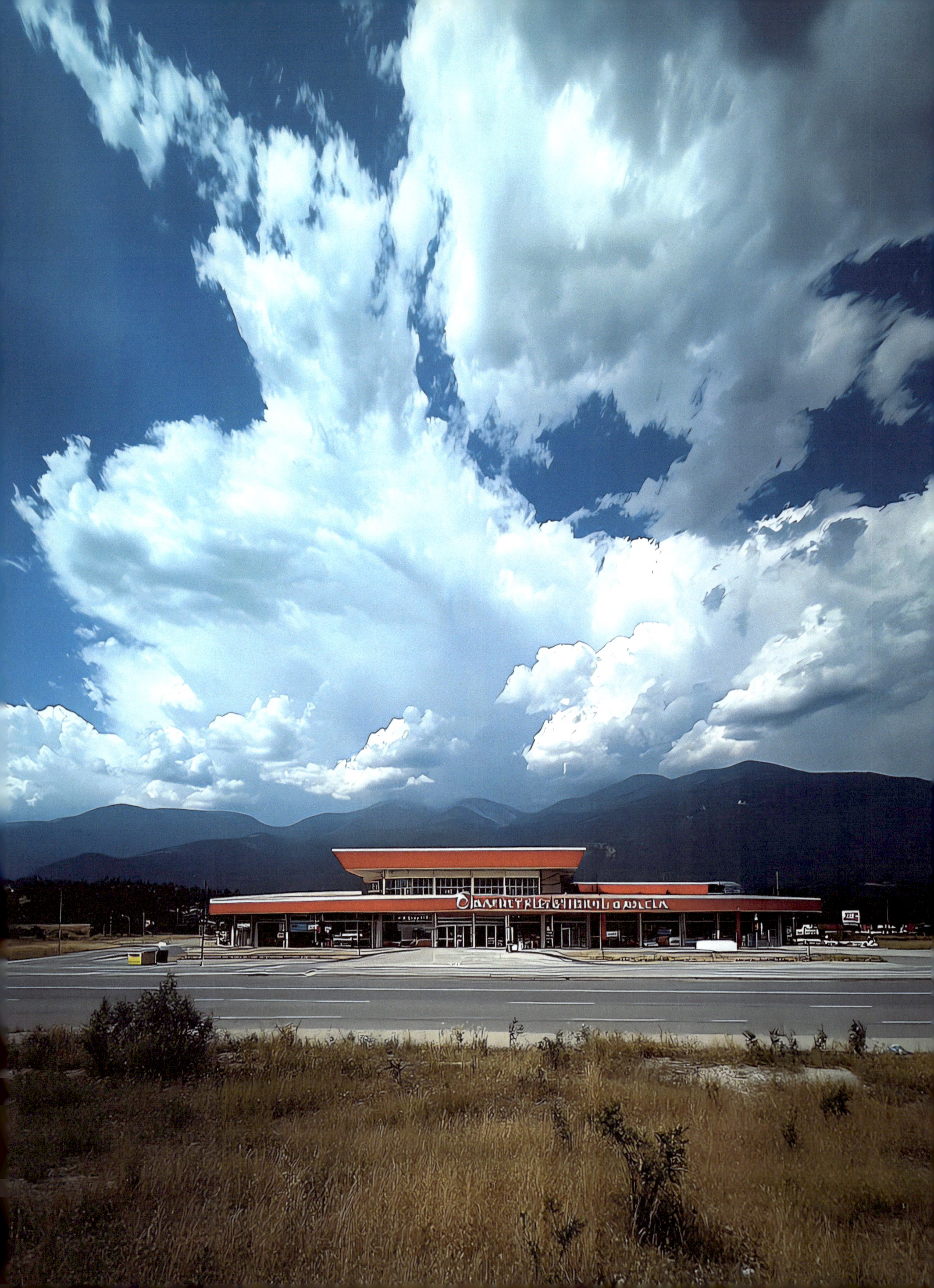

www.ingramcontent.com/pod-product-compliance
Lightning Source LLC
Chambersburg PA
CBHW040420220526
45473CB00004B/1302
* 9 7 9 8 3 0 3 3 4 1 2 8 9 *